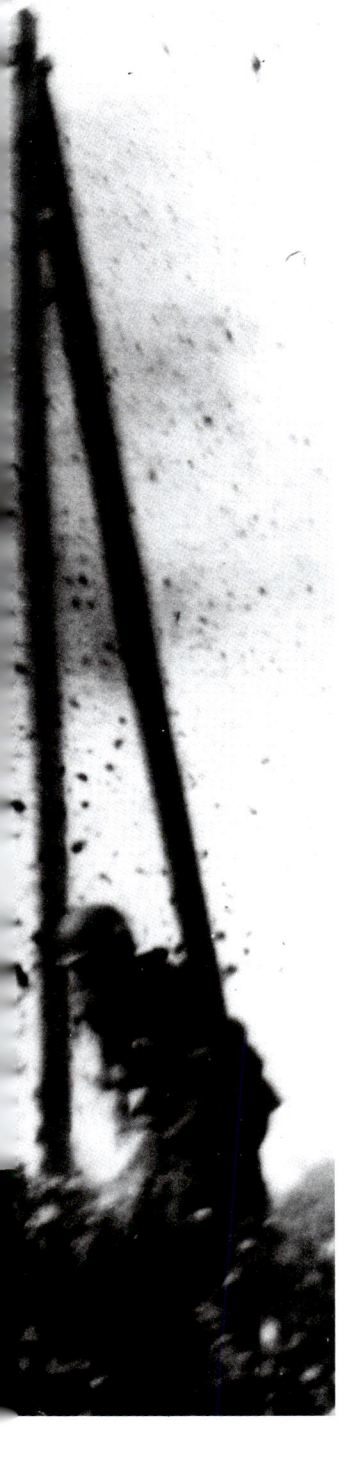

HELL'S HIGHWAY

THE TRUE STORY OF THE 101ST AIRBORNE DIVISION DURING OPERATION MARKET GARDEN, SEPTEMBER 17–25, 1944

JOHN ANTAL

Foreword by Gorge E. Koskimaki, WWII Screaming Eagle veteran

ZENITH PRESS

To the U.S. Army, those who serve, and especially to the soldiers of the 101st Airborne in World War II.

Special thanks to Dr. Frances Antal, loving mother, educator, and U.S. Air Force veteran, who instilled in me a desire to read and a thirst for history.

First published in 2008 by Zenith Press, an imprint of MBI Publishing Company, 400 First Avenue North, Suite 300, Minneapolis, MN 55401 USA

Copyright © 2008 by Gearbox Software, LLC

MBI Publishing Company titles are also available at discounts in bulk quantity for industrial or sales-promotional use. For details write to Special Sales Manager at MBI Publishing Company, 400 First Avenue North, Suite 300, Minneapolis, MN 55401 USA

Library of Congress Cataloging-in-Publication Data

Antal, John F., 1955–
  Hell's Highway : the true story of the 101st Airborne Division during Operation Market Garden, September 17-25, 1944 / John Antal.
    p. cm.
  Includes bibliographical references.
  ISBN-13: 978-0-7603-3348-8 (pbk. : alk. paper)
  1. Arnhem, Battle of, Arnhem, Netherlands, 1944. 2. United States. Army. Airborne Division, 101st—History. 3. World War, 1939–1945—Regimental histories—United States. I. Title.
  D763.N42A7235 2008
  940.54'219218—dc22

                                      2008019725

Art Direction: Brian Donahue
Layout by: Brenda C. Canales
Maps by: Jason Petho, pethocarto@techemail.com

Printed in Singapore

On the cover: 101st Airborne paratroopers move past a burning truck in the town of Veghel. The Americans were desperate to reopen Hell's Highway as the British Airborne at Arnhem suffered terribly under German counterattacks. *U.S. Army photo*

On the frontispiece: Private First Class Park H. Appler, G Company, 506th Parachute Infantry Regiment, saunters off the Son drop zone and walks past happy Dutch civilians on September 17, 1944. Note the gliders circling to land in the air behind him. This paratrooper carries an M1903 Springfield rifle that has been adapted to shoot rifle grenades. *U.S. Army photo*

On the title pages: On October 5, 1944, the 101st Airborne Division moved north to take up defensive positions in the British line, in an area known as "the island." This area, a narrow strip of land north of Nijmegen, situated between the lower Rhine and Waal rivers, was subjected to heavy German shelling. *U.S. Army photo*

On the back cover: Brigadier General Anthony McAuliffe, the assistant division commander, 101st Airborne Division, briefs C-47 and glider pilots before taking off from England to reinforce the 101st on September 18, 1944. *U.S. Army photo*

About the Author:

John Antal, Colonel, U.S. Army (Ret.), spent thirty years on active duty, commanding combat soldiers at every level from platoon to regiment while stationed in Germany, Korea, Kuwait, and the United States. Antal is a graduate of West Point, was an Airborne Ranger, and has earned the Expert Infantryman's Badge. In 2003 he was founding editorial director of *Armchair General* magazine, where he continues today as a contributing editor. He currently serves as Vice President of Knowledge Operations at Gearbox Software of Plano, Texas, where he is the staff military historian and advisor. Antal has published seven books, contributed to several military anthologies, and written over fifty magazine articles. He has appeared on episodes of A&E's *Brute Force* and the History Channel's *Weapons at War*, and, in 2005, co-directed *Brothers in Arms: The Untold Story of the 502* for the History Channel. He also wrote the first *Brothers in Arms* companion novel, *Brothers in Arms: Hell's Highway*.

Contents

Foreword

George Koskimaki

SIXTY-THREE YEARS AGO, as a member of the 101st Airborne Division, the "Screaming Eagles," I participated in the largest airborne operation in military history, Operation Market Garden, the invasion of Holland. This operation was designed to shorten the war and to free the people of the Netherlands from Nazi occupation.

The battle for Hell's Highway is a story that should be remembered. The story is one of sacrifice and battle, a story of paratroopers who fought against difficult odds and pulled through due to their courage and faith in one another.

Operation Market Garden was a bold attempt to end the war in 1944. During nine days of courageous fighting, the young men of the United States and the British 2nd Army fought to keep a narrow stretch of highway open in order to pierce the German defenses from the Belgium border to the Rhine. The American 101st Airborne and 82nd Airborne divisions accomplished their missions, but not without great loss in casualties. The British XXX Corps fought through the 101st and 82nd Airborne division areas in a desperate and gallant attempt to reach the British 1st Airborne and Polish Brigade at Arnhem. That the British and Polish paratroopers were not reached in time is one of the great tragedies of World War II; the term *a bridge too far* is now a part of our lexicon because of this heroic effort.

This book by Col. John Antal is a fitting tribute to the men of the Screaming Eagle Division. In maps, photos, authentic reenactment photographs, and screenshots from the Gearbox Software game *Hell's Highway*, you are offered a rare glimpse of a distant time and place. As a veteran of Operation Market Garden, I recommend this book as a testimony to the courage and sacrifice of the soldiers of the 101st Airborne Division and to all who fought in this operation to bring an end to Nazism.

—George Koskimaki
World War II veteran and technical sergeant, U.S. Army
101st Airborne Division

Preface

Hell's Highway is about the 101st Airborne Division during Operation Market Garden. This book explains the day-to-day battles in maps, photos, veterans' interviews, photo reenactments, and computer-generated art, offering a vivid glimpse into a fascinating and dramatic chapter in history. As you will see in the following chapters, the plan to seize a crossing over the Rhine and end the war by Christmas 1944 failed, but the courage of the troops who fought in Operation Market Garden was never in question.

Hell's Highway is also intended as a companion book to Gearbox Software's video game *Brothers in Arms: Hell's Highway* and presents the true history of the battle. The pages that follow will provide anyone experiencing the *Hell's Highway* video game with a detailed glimpse at the real history of the battle. The actions of the 101st Airborne Division are explained with text, maps, historical photos, reenactment photos, and *Brothers in Arms: Hell's Highway* screenshots.

Operation Market Garden was the largest airborne operation in the history of warfare and included the actions of the 101st Airborne Division, the 82nd Airborne Division, the British 1st Airborne Division, the Polish Airborne Brigade, the British XXX Corps, and many other Allied and Axis military units. The actions of these units are discussed in this book only in their relation to the 101st Airborne Division.

The information from this book has been collected from a large variety of sources, including walking the battlefields where the fighting actually took place and talking with hundreds of veterans of the battle. The primary source material was derived from official U.S. Army studies, pamphlets, and reports. The historical photographs are primarily from the U.S. Army Signal Corps taken during the battle. Reenactment photos are provided to highlight authentic weapons, uniforms, and equipment. Video game screenshots are used to show how interactive experiences like the video game *Brothers in Arms: Hell's Highway* can bring history alive to a new generation of people.

— *John Antal*
biabooks@gmail.com

European Theatre

June 1941

Nazi Germany

Axis Occupied Area
Spain

Soviet Union

Neutral

N

0   100   200 miles

0   100   200   300 kilometers

Petho Cartography 2008

IRELAND

UNITED KINGDOM

NORWAY

SWEDEN

FINLAND

North Sea

DENMARK

Baltic Sea

ESTONIA

LATVIA

LITHUANIA

SOVIET UNION

HOLLAND

BELGIUM

LUX

EAST PRUSSIA

GERMANY

POLAND

FRANCE

SWITZ

SLOVAKIA

HUNGARY

ROMANIA

SPAIN

ANDORA

YUGOSLAVIA

BULGARIA

Black Sea

Corsica

ITALY

Mallorca

Menorca

Eivissa

Sardina

ALBANIA

GREECE

TURKEY

Sicily

MALTA

Mediterranean Sea

Crete

LYBIA

EGYPT

CHAPTER 1

The Screaming Eagles

IN 1939, when Hitler's Germany invaded Poland, starting World War II, the U.S. Army was ill-equipped, untrained, and unprepared to fight against well-trained and well-equipped military forces on a global scale. The Germans demonstrated success in waging a style of war that was dramatically different than the method and tempo of World War I. In this new German method of fighting, fast-moving tank forces supported by air forces, paratroopers, infantry, and artillery were choreographed by a well-trained and well-disciplined command system that employed rapid decision making. The result in 1939 and 1940 was one of the most successful examples of combined arms warfare in history and rapid triumph for the Germans.

Where is the Prince who can afford so to cover his country with troops for its defense, as that 10,000 men descending from the clouds might not, in many places, do an infinite deal of mischief before a force could be brought together to repel them?

—Benjamin Franklin, 1784

A paratrooper wearing his parachute and using a walkie-talkie stands next to a C-47 aircraft in 1942. *U.S. Army photo*

The Birth of the American Airborne

AS THE GERMAN BLITZKRIEG chalked up victory after victory in the early months of World War II, the Germans' employment of paratrooper and glider forces caught the imagination of military planners in the United States. The idea, as Benjamin Franklin prophesized in the eighteenth century, of "men descending from the clouds" had been realized. Airborne advocates in the U.S. Army argued that landing large numbers of skilled infantrymen by parachute and glider behind enemy lines was essential to win in modern war. It was clear that if paratroopers could be flown over enemy lines and dropped behind their defenses, the attacker would gain a powerful tactical advantage. The ability of airborne forces to land anywhere behind enemy lines within range of their transport aircraft would force the enemy to spread their defenses to protect less-defended rear areas. The decisive use of paratrooper and glider units by the Germans in Holland in 1940 and Crete in 1941 proved the airborne concept and provided the spark for the creation of airborne forces in the U.S. Army.

To assess the airborne concept, the U.S. Army formed an airborne test platoon in June 1940. First Lieutenant William T. Ryder, the platoon leader of the U.S. Army airborne test platoon, made his first parachute jump from a U.S. military aircraft on August 16, 1940, at

Members of the 506th Parachute Infantry Regiment doing pull-ups during their early training at Camp Toccoa, Georgia, in the fall of 1942.

U.S. Army photo

BLOOD UPON THE RISERS*

He was just a rookie trooper, and he surely shook with fright
As he checked all his equipment and made sure his pack was tight.
He had to sit and listen to those awful engines roar,
"You ain't gonna jump no more!"
(Chorus)

Gory, gory, what a helluva way to die!
Gory, gory, what a helluva way to die!
Gory, gory, what a helluva way to die!
And he ain't gonna jump no more!

"Is everybody happy!" cried the sergeant looking up.
Our hero meekly answered, "Yes," and then they stood him up.
He jumped into the icy blast, his static line unhooked,
And he ain't gonna jump no more!
(Chorus)

He counted loud, he counted long, he waited for the shock.
He felt the wind, he felt the clouds, he felt that awful drop.
The silk from his reserve fell out and wrapped about his legs,
And he ain't gonna jump no more!
(Chorus)

The risers wrapped around his neck, connectors cracked his dome,
Suspension lines were tied in knots around his skinny bones.
His canopy became a shroud as he hurtled to the ground,
And he ain't gonna jump no more!
(Chorus)

The days he lived and loved and laughed kept running through his mind,
He thought about the girl back home, the one he'd left behind.
He thought about the medics, and he wondered what they'd find,
And he ain't gonna jump no more!
(Chorus)

The ambulance was on the spot and jeeps were running wild
The medics jumped and screamed with glee, rolled up their sleeves and smiled.
For it had been a week or so since last a chute had failed,
And he ain't gonna jump no more!
(Chorus)

He hit the ground, the sound was *splat*, the blood went spurting high.
His comrades then were heard to say: "A helluva way to die!"
He lay there rolling 'round in all the welter of his gore,
And he ain't gonna jump no more!
(Chorus)

There was blood upon the risers, there were brains upon his chute.
Intestines were a-danglin' from his paratrooper suit.
They poured him from his helmet and poured him from his boots,
And he ain't gonna jump no more!
(Chorus)

Sung to the tune of "The Battle Hymn of the Republic." This is just one of many variations of the song, which originated with American paratroopers of World War II.

The last lap of the 506th Parachute Infantry Regiment's "torture course" at Camp Toccoa, Georgia, in the fall of 1942.
U.S. Army photo

Lawson Field, Fort Benning, Georgia, from a B-18 Bolo bomber. He was immediately followed by Pvt. William N. King, the first enlisted soldier to make a parachute jump. Pleased with the performance of the test platoon, the unit was expanded several months later, and the 501st Parachute Battalion was organized as a permanent airborne infantry unit.

Three additional parachute battalions were subsequently organized and placed under the administrative control of the Provisional Parachute Group, commanded by Lt. Col. William C. Lee. Lee had studied the German innovations in airborne warfare and was a fierce advocate for the airborne concept in the U.S. Army. He had served as an infantry officer in World War I, graduated from the American and French tank schools in 1929–1930, and later served as a military attaché in France and Great Britain. Lee supervised the work of the U.S. Army Test Platoon at Fort Benning, Georgia, and activated the Provisional Parachute Group in 1941.

Paratroopers jump from a C-47 transport aircraft to test the concept of landing airborne troops behind enemy lines. *U.S. Army photo*

The Parachute Infantry Regiments (PIRs)

AS THE AIRBORNE PROGRAM GREW, the army created airborne organization, tactics, and doctrine. The army quickly recognized that the organization for large-scale combat deployments required the formation of battalions, regiments, and divisions. In February 1942, four parachute infantry regiments (PIRs) were created and

THE AIRBORNE CREED

I am an Airborne trooper, a paratrooper! I jump by parachute from any plane in flight. I volunteered to do it, knowing well the hazards off my choice. I serve in a mighty Airborne force, famed in deeds in war and renowned for readiness in peace. I pledge to uphold its honor and prestige in all I am and all I do. I am an elite trooper, a sky trooper, a shock trooper, a spearhead trooper. I blaze the way to far flung goals behind, before, above the foe's front line. I know that I have to fight without support for days on end. Therefore, I keep mind and body always fit to do my part in any Airborne task. I am self-reliant and unafraid. I shoot true and march fast and far. I fight hard and execute in every art and artifice of war. I never fail a fellow trooper. I cherish as a sacred trust the lives of the men with whom I serve. Leaders have my fullest loyalty, and those I lead never find me lacking. I have pride in the Airborne! I never let it down. In peace, I do not shirk the dullest duty nor protest the toughest training. My weapons and equipment are always combat ready. I am neat of dress, military in courtesy, proper in conduct and behavior. In battle, I fear no foe's ability, nor underestimate his prowess, power, and agility. I fight him with all my might and skill ever alert to evade capture or escape a trap. I never surrender, though I may be the last. My goal in peace and war is to succeed in any mission of the day or die if it needs be in the try. I belong to a proud and glorious team, the Airborne, the army, my country. I am its chosen pride to fight where others may not go to serve them well until the final victory.

I am the Airborne!

General Order Number Five

The 101st Airborne Division, activated at Camp Claiborne, Louisiana, has no history, but it has a rendezvous with destiny. Like the early American pioneers whose invincible courage was the foundation stone of this nation, we have broken with the past and its traditions in order to establish our claim to the future.

Due to the nature of our armament, and the tactics in which we shall perfect ourselves, we shall be called upon to carry out operations of far-reaching military importance and we shall habitually go into action when the need is immediate and extreme.

Let me call your attention to the fact that our badge is the great American eagle. This is a fitting emblem for a division that will crush its enemies by falling upon them like a thunderbolt from the skies.

The history we shall make, the record of high achievement we hope to write in the annals of the American Army and the American people, depends wholly and completely on the men of this division. Each individual, each officer and each enlisted man, must therefore regard himself as a necessary part of a complex and powerful instrument for the overcoming of the enemies of the nation. Each, in his own job, must realize that he is not only a means, but an indispensable means for obtaining the goal of victory. It is, therefore, not too much to say that the future itself, in whose molding we expect to have our share, is in the hands of the soldiers of the 101st Airborne Division.

Members of the 506th Parachute Infantry Regiment pay close attention to the potential paratrooper exiting from the thirty-four-foot tower at Camp Toccoa, Georgia, in the fall of 1942. *U.S. Army photo*

Soldiers shaking out parachutes at the Airborne School, Fort Benning, Georgia. *U.S. Army photo*

consolidated with the existing parachute battalions. The following month the Airborne Command was created to oversee the training of the parachute regiments.

The development of glider infantry, another type of airborne unit, coincided with the growth of the parachute forces. This mix of glider and parachute regiments was a matter of great debate and would change as the airborne concept matured. The airborne organization initially consisted of a mix of glider infantry regiments (GIRs) and PIRs. Glider troops would be expected to land on airfields or other designated landing zones that were first secured by paratroopers. Artillery, heavy equipment, and supplies would also be flown in by gliders. Organized as "infantry airborne battalions," the glider units

The three-hundred-foot tower at the Airborne School at Fort Benning, Georgia, provided paratrooper recruits the opportunity to test their courage and skill. *U.S. Army photo*

Training in the United States

Here you met guys from all over. Got your first glimpse of tent city . . . and learned that the whistle at 5:45 a.m. meant to be ready to fall out in exactly ten minutes. And what a place that was! So hot that you sweated like you had never sweat before. The weather was absolutely unpredictable. One moment it would be fair and sunny, the next it would be pouring down rain. How it did it no one knows. The water came from apparently cloudless skies. There was always something to be done. If you weren't busy drilling, the first sergeant could always be depended on to keep you busy at something else. Details were one thing you hated, so invariably you got the worst of them. You were still green at this army game and dumb enough to work hard. Sometimes. But, oh my! How we could get tangled up in those salutes. You always had a cigarette in your mouth or in the right hand.

From that day, we were taught the fine art of foot dril. We learned to stand at attention when speaking to an officer, to be sure and say Sir, and to never, under any circumstances, fail to salute. Day after day it was "Right face, left face, about face, forward march, and halt." On and on, ad nauseam. Always each hour came that welcome, "Take a break." We become efficient in getting those pup-tents up and taking them down. It was pretty hard driving the pegs in that hard-packed drill field. How to adjust a pack, how to roll the bed roll, all were learned in record time. Even our instructors were elated at our aptitude.

You gradually caught on that in the army you would line up for everything. Later in your career you were destined to call it "Queing."

At the end no one ever had a nickel for the "Coke" machine, or if there was a nickel there was no Coke.

A few weeks passed, you were getting toughened up a bit, so one day a hike was scheduled. Five miles. "Holy smoke," you thought, "I'll never make it." You did, though. After you reached the end, and everybody was expecting a kind of party that night, it was your luck that the first sergeant picked you and a couple of other guys to dig a latrine. By the time you were through digging, there was barely time enough before dark to pitch your tent.

Besides being so tired that you weren't in the least interested in the hilarity going on over by the Gravel Pit. There really must have been some fun, though, because the crowd could be heard for miles with their shouting and laughing. You were more concerned with getting a place on this hard ground where you could stretch out and relax. You still hadn't figured out why the first sergeant had picked on you. Boy, was it hot the next day, as you were going back into camp. Your feet were blistered and you had half a mind to get into the ambulance that was tailing the battalion. You knew that if you did that you would feel like a sissy, so you walked and suffered. Just before you reached camp, it started to rain and everyone got drenched. What a day![1]

British Field Marshall Sir John Dill (far left) and Gen. George C. Marshall, chief of staff, U.S. Army, (right) inspect a platoon of the 502nd Parachute Infantry Regiment in the spring of 1942. Between them is Brig. Gen. William C. Lee, commanding general, U.S. Airborne Command. *U.S. Army photo*

Doing sit-ups on the bars, the U.S. Army Airborne way, at the Fort Benning, Georgia, Airborne School in 1943. *U.S. Army photo*

A demolition squad from the 502nd Parachute Infantry Regiment prepares to blow a bridge in the Tennessee maneuver area on June 8, 1943.

U.S. Army photo

existed and trained separately from the parachute battalions.

Rivalries between the paratrooper and glider units grew as the new organization was formed. Part of the problem was the status, and extra pay was given to paratroopers but denied to glider men. The paratroopers were considered to be elite troops and received extra money or "parachute pay" for their hazardous missions. The glider troops, however, had duties that were just as dangerous—if not more so—but were authorized no extra pay. This situation continued through 1944, with unit commanders doing their best to keep the peace within their ranks.

The 101st Airborne Division Trains for War

IN AUGUST 1942, the 101st Airborne Division was activated at Camp Claiborne, Louisiana, with recently promoted Maj. Gen. William C. Lee commanding. In his first address to his soldiers, Maj. Gen. William C. Lee of the 101st Airborne Division declared prophetically in General Order Number 5, dated August 19, 1942, that "the 101st Airborne

MAXWELL DAVENPORT TAYLOR

Taylor was born in Keytesville, Missouri, on August 26, 1901, and graduated from the U.S. Military Academy in 1922, commissioned as a second lieutenant of engineering. He studied French in Paris and was an instructor in French and later Spanish at West Point, 1927–1932. Taylor was also a student of Japanese at the American embassy in Tokyo, 1935–1939, with detached military attaché duty at Peking, China, in 1937. Graduating from the Army War College in 1940, he served in the Office of the Secretary of the General Staff, 1941–1942.

Taylor's rise to the highest echelons of U.S. government began under the tutelage of Gen. Matthew B. Ridgeway in the U.S. Army's 82nd Airborne Division when Ridgeway commanded the division in the early part of World War II. Taylor served as the 82nd's chief of staff, 1942, then its artillery commander in operations in Sicily and Italy, 1942–1944.

In 1943, his diplomatic and language skills resulted in a secret mission to Rome to coordinate an 82nd air drop with Italian forces. He met with the new Italian prime minister, Marshal Pietro Badoglio. The air drop near Rome to capture the city was called off at the last minute, when Taylor realized that it was too late. German forces were already moving in to cover the intended drop zones. Transport planes were already in the air when Taylor's message cancelled the drop, preventing the suicide mission. These efforts behind enemy lines got Taylor noticed at the highest levels of the Allied command.

After the campaigns in the Mediterranean, Taylor was assigned to the 101st Airborne Division, which was training in England. After the 101st's founder and commander, Maj. Gen. Bill Lee, suffered a heart attack, Taylor was given command of the division, receiving a temporary promotion to major general in May 1944. He commanded the 101st Airborne Division through the Normandy invasion and the western European campaigns, 1944–1945.

Major General Maxwell D. Taylor, the commander of the U.S. 101st Airborne Division, was ordered to land his division in two locations just north of the British XXX Corps in order to take the bridges northwest of Eindhoven at Son and Veghel. General Taylor took off from Welford airfield in England and jumped with the 1st Battalion, 502nd Parachute Infantry Regiment. *U.S. Army photo*

Taylor jumped into Normandy on June 5, 1944, with his men. He was the first Allied general to land in France on D-Day. Although he held command of the 101st Airborne Division for the rest of the war, he missed out leading the division during its most famous conflict, the Battle of Bastogne, during the Battle of the Bulge, because he was attending a staff conference in the United States. General Anthony McAuliffe assumed command of the division. Some of the paratroopers resented Taylor for this later.

Following the war, he was superintendent of West Point, 1945–1949, then commander of Allied troops in Berlin, 1949–1951. In 1953, he was sent to the Korean War as commander of the Eighth Army in the final operations of the war. He was chief of staff of the U.S. Army, 1955–1959, succeeding his former mentor, Matthew B. Ridgeway. During 1957, President Dwight D. Eisenhower ordered General Taylor to deploy a thousand troops from the 101st Airborne Division to Little Rock, Arkansas, to enforce federal court orders to desegregate Central High School during the Little Rock Crisis.

Taylor opposed dependence upon a massive retaliation doctrine, pushed for an increase in conventional forces to ensure a capability of flexible response, guided the transition to a Pentomic structure for infantry divisions, and directed army participation in sensitive operations at Lebanon, Taiwan, and Berlin. He retired from active service in July 1959.

On October 1, 1962, President Kennedy appointed Taylor as chairman of the Joint Chiefs of Staff. In 1964 he again retired from the army, becoming ambassador to South Vietnam, 1964–1965, succeeding Henry Cabot Lodge Jr. Taylor was special consultant to the president and chairman of the Foreign Intelligence Advisory Board, 1965–1969, and president of the Institute of Defense Analysis, 1966–1969. General Taylor died in Washington, D.C., on April 19, 1987, of Lou Gehrig's disease. He was interred at Arlington National Cemetery.

Division, which was activated on August 16, 1942, at Camp Claiborne, Louisiana, has no history, but it has a rendezvous with destiny." Thus begins the storied history of one of the U.S. Army's finest combat divisions.

As soon as the 101st was designated as an airborne division, Lee began training his soldiers for combat operations. The 101st then moved to Fort Bragg, North Carolina, in October 1942 and was joined by the 502nd PIR.

The division's first test came in 1943 during the Tennessee maneuvers. One of the lessons learned from the Tennessee maneuvers was experienced by a parachute rifle company that would find itself in a similar situation in September 1944, during Operation Market Garden.

Airborne leaders. Pictured from left to right are: Brig. Gen. Joseph Swing (82nd Airborne Division Artillery), Maj. Gen. Matthew Ridgeway (commanding general, 82nd Airborne Division), Maj. Gen. William C. Lee (commanding general, 101st Airborne Division), and Brigadier General Chapman in 1943. *U.S. Army photo*

On the first day of the Tennessee maneuvers, the company marched fifteen miles across country to capture a bridge that they were given a week to capture. Shortly after capturing the bridge, they spent a week defending it, surrounded and cut off from food and support.

The 101st Airborne Division excelled during the Tennessee maneuvers and dramatically demonstrated the capabilities of the airborne division. During these maneuvers, however, General Lee was injured in a glider. He later remarked: "Next time I'll take a parachute," which provided the overlooked glider troops with some measure of satisfaction, if not extra pay.

The Screaming Eagles then returned to Fort Bragg and continued to train for combat. Everyone in the division knew that the invasion of Europe was imminent, and training was intensified in small-unit tactical operations, weapons, and demolitions training. The division was transferred by ship to England in late 1943. Arriving in England, the 101st was quartered in Wiltshire and Berkshire, where the division conducted more combat training. In January, the 101st Airborne received its third parachute regiment, the 501st PIR. The division now consisted of three parachute infantry regiments (the 501st, 502nd, and 506th) and one glider infantry regiment (the 327th) as its main infantry elements.

Change of Command

ON FEBRUARY 5, 1944, General Lee, who had championed the airborne cause from the beginning, suffered a heart attack. Although he had brought the division from its initial organization through training for the fight in Europe, and was highly respected by his soldiers and superiors, General Lee was not to be part of the 101st's

baptism of fire. His medical condition precluded his continued role as commander of the Screaming Eagles. As a result, Lee was relieved of his command and returned to the United States.

His replacement was Brig. Gen. Maxwell D. Taylor. Taylor was an airborne veteran of the 82nd Airborne's operations in Sicily and Italy and was the former commander of the 82nd Airborne Division Artillery. Taylor had proven himself to be a talented and adaptive officer. In 1943, Taylor's diplomatic and language skills were put to the test when he was assigned a secret mission to Rome.

This mission occurred when the Italians were about to switch sides from the Axis Powers to the Allied cause. To secure Rome during this switch, Allied planners wanted to drop the 82nd Airborne Division to occupy Rome with the help of Italian forces. Taylor was sent behind enemy lines to Rome to coordinate the parachute drop of the 82nd Airborne Division and met with the new Italian prime minister, Marshal Pietro Badoglio. Taylor soon discovered that the Italians had lost control of the situation, and their surrender to the Allies was being stopped by the Germans. German forces were already moving to cover potential drop zones and were rapidly disarming the Italian army. At the last minute, with American C-47 transport aircraft already in flight, Taylor sent a message to cancel the drop, thus preventing the destruction of the 82nd Airborne Division.

Taylor assumed command of the 101st on March 14, 1944. The final organizational change prior to D-Day occurred when the 1st Battalion, 401st GIR, was transferred from the 82nd Airborne Division to the 101st Division and attached to the 327th GIR to operate under that regiment as a third battalion. The 1st Battalion, 401st GIR, was made an official element of the 327th GIR in April 1945.

The training of the 101st Airborne Division continued from March through May 1944 as the invasion of Europe loomed. The organization and tactics were set. Now, it was time to test the division in combat.

The Airborne is ready for war. Members of the 502nd Parachute Infantry Regiment passing in review on April 10, 1943. *U.S. Army photo*

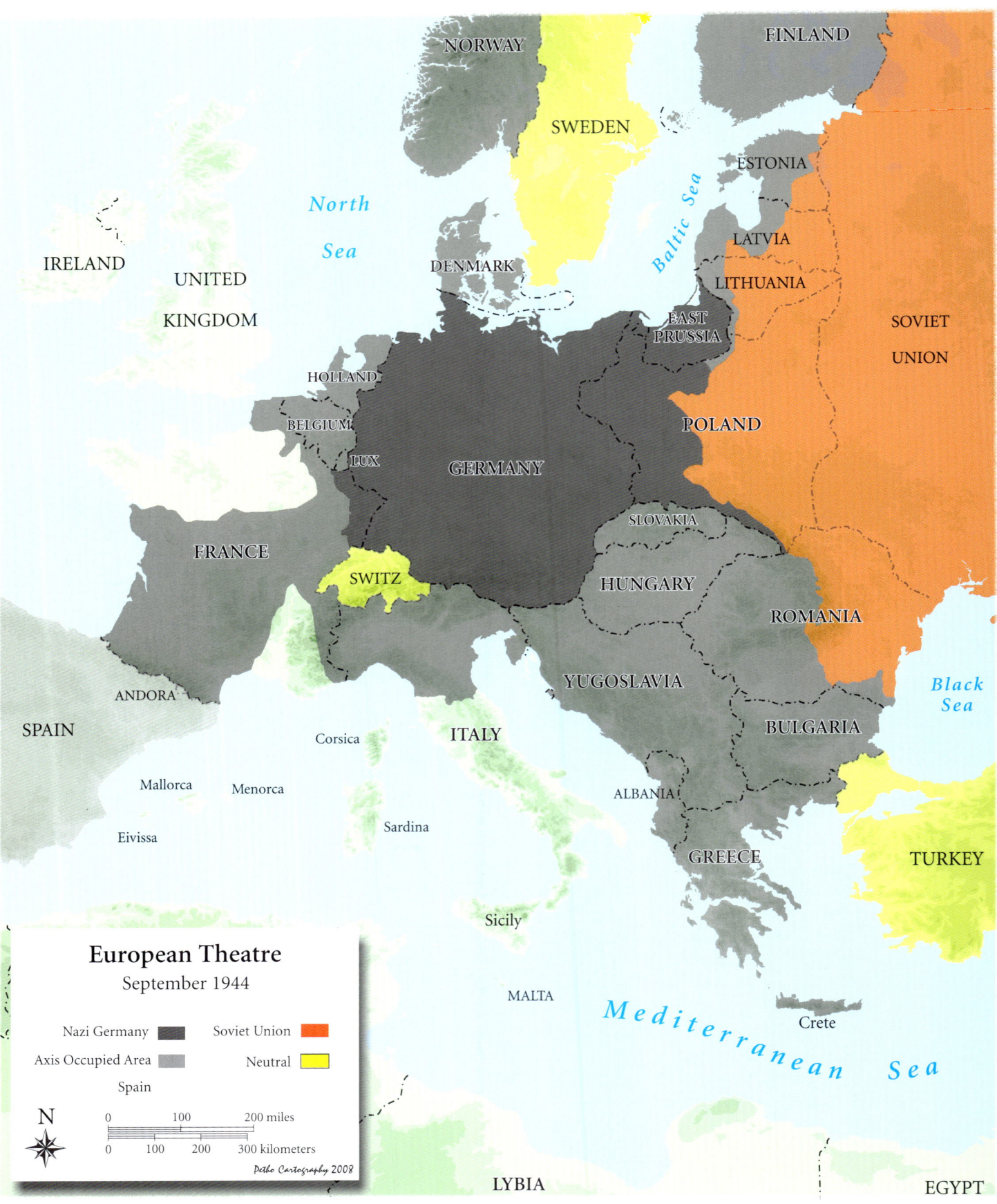

NORWAY

FINLAND

SWEDEN

North Sea

ESTONIA

Baltic Sea

IRELAND

UNITED KINGDOM

DENMARK

LATVIA

LITHUANIA

SOVIET UNION

EAST PRUSSIA

HOLLAND

POLAND

BELGIUM

LUX

GERMANY

SLOVAKIA

FRANCE

SWITZ

HUNGARY

ROMANIA

Black Sea

YUGOSLAVIA

ANDORA

BULGARIA

SPAIN

Corsica

ITALY

Mallorca

Menorca

ALBANIA

Eivissa

Sardina

GREECE

TURKEY

Sicily

MALTA

Mediterranean Sea

Crete

European Theatre

September 1944

Nazi Germany

Soviet Union

Axis Occupied Area

Neutral

Spain

N

| 0 | 100 | 200 miles |

| 0 | 100 | 200 | 300 kilometers |

Petho Cartography 2008

LYBIA

EGYPT

CHAPTER 2

The Invasion of Europe

THE 101ST AIRBORNE Division had transferred to England for one purpose: to spearhead the invasion of France. Training for D-Day in England, the 101st participated in three formal exercises—Beaver, Tiger, and Eagle—to prepare for their D-Day mission. The last exercise, Operation Eagle, was held during the second week of May as a dress rehearsal for the invasion. The paratroopers of the 101st jumped from C-47 transport aircraft to capture the causeways leading away from a simulated beach. During Eagle, most of the 101st was dropped on the wrong coordinates, but the mission was accomplished, and the exercise was considered a success. With D-Day set for early June, the Screaming Eagles returned to their camp to make final preparations before D-Day.

Corporal Louis E. Laird, 101st Airborne Division, stands in the door of a Douglas C-47 Skytrain during rehearsals prior to D-Day. As part of his equipment, he has an M9 60mm Bazooka slung over his shoulder. *U.S. Army photo*

I am no ordinary soldier-king but a warlord . . . probably the most successful in history.

—Adolf Hitler, 1943

It was now just a question of time—and lives.

—German Field Marshal Gerd von Rundstedt, commander in chief, West, after the successful Allied invasion at Normandy

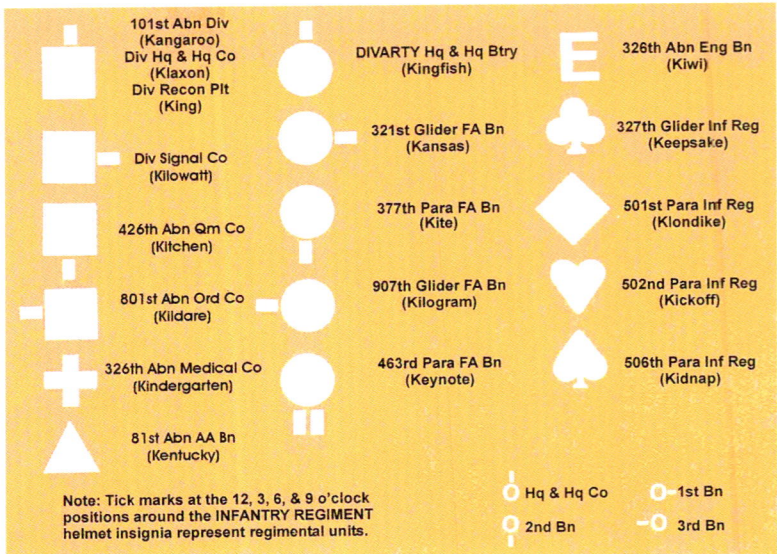

101st Abn Div (Kangaroo) Div Hq & Hq Co (Klaxon) Div Recon Plt (King)	DIVARTY Hq & Hq Btry (Kingfish)	326th Abn Eng Bn (Kiwi)
Div Signal Co (Kilowatt)	321st Glider FA Bn (Kansas)	327th Glider Inf Reg (Keepsake)
426th Abn Qm Co (Kitchen)	377th Para FA Bn (Kite)	501st Para Inf Reg (Klondike)
801st Abn Ord Co (Kildare)	907th Glider FA Bn (Kilogram)	502nd Para Inf Reg (Kickoff)
326th Abn Medical Co (Kindergarten)	463rd Para FA Bn (Keynote)	506th Para Inf Reg (Kidnap)
81st Abn AA Bn (Kentucky)		

Note: Tick marks at the 12, 3, 6, & 9 o'clock positions around the INFANTRY REGIMENT helmet insignia represent regimental units.

Hq & Hq Co — 1st Bn
2nd Bn — 3rd Bn

This chart depicts the helmet markings of the units of the 101st Airborne Division. Each regiment and the support battalions had a symbol stenciled in white paint on the left and right side of the helmet.

U.S. Army photo

AT 2215 HOURS ON JUNE 5, 1944, D–1, 6,600 paratroops of the 101st Airborne Division started taking off in 432 C-47 transport aircraft from seven separate airfields in England. They were scheduled to begin dropping in France shortly after midnight. At dawn (H–2 hours) they were to be reinforced by approximately 150 glider troops from fifty-one gliders, and at dusk (H+15 hours) by an additional 165 in thirty-two gliders. Twenty pathfinder aircraft preceded the main echelons by a half hour. The Pathfinders' mission was to mark the drop zones for the night landings. At 0015 in the darkness of June 6, 1944, Capt. Frank L. Lillyman, the leader of the 101st Pathfinders, became the first Allied soldier to touch French soil.

The division, as part of the VII Corps assault, was assigned the task of seizing positions west of Utah Beach. Given the mission of anchoring the corps' southern flank, the division was also to eliminate the Germans' secondary beach defenses, allowing the seaborne forces of the 4th Infantry Division, once ashore, to continue inland. The Screaming Eagles were to capture the causeway bridges that ran behind the beach between St. Martin-de-Varreville and Pouppeville. In the division's southern sector, the Screaming Eagles were to seize the La Barquette lock and destroy a highway bridge northwest of the town of Carentan and a railroad bridge farther west. At the same time, elements of the division were to establish two bridgeheads on the Douve River at Le Port, northeast of Carentan.

CRACKING HITLER'S ATLANTIC WALL

General Eisenhower made a fateful decision on June 5, 1944: to proceed with the invasion that would crack open Hitler's Atlantic Wall and free the people of Europe. The Allies had waited nearly four years for this opportunity, and Eisenhower knew that he would get only one chance to get it right. During the night of June 5, more than five thousand ships moved toward the beaches. At two o'clock on the morning of June 6, one British and two U.S. Airborne divisions (the 82nd and 101st Airborne divisions) dropped behind the beaches to secure routes of egress for the seaborne forces. Following preliminary aerial and naval bombardment, the first waves of infantry and tanks began to touch down at 6:30, just after sunrise. Some fifty thousand U.S. troops made their way ashore on Omaha and Utah beaches before the day was out. The British and Canadians landed on Gold, Juno, and Sword beaches. American casualties were approximately 6,500, British and Canadian 3,000—in both cases lighter than expected. The German command was slow to react to the invasion, having been misled not only by the bad weather across Normandy but also by an Allied deception plan that continued to deceive Hitler and lead him to believe that the Normandy invasion was only a diversionary assault and that the main landings were to come later on the Pas de Calais. The Allies cracked Hitler's Atlantic Wall and were on the continent of Europe to stay. From this point forward, the Allies would move forward toward Germany until victory was won.

LIVING IN ENGLAND WITH THE 321st

We certainly weren't much impressed when we viewed Whatcombe Farm for the first time. [The 321st Glider Field Artillery Battalion had first arrived in England in mid-September 1943.] However, we were in no condition to have an unprejudiced opinion of anything English. Having ridden all night on one of those "Dinky" Limey trains, all the way from Liverpool, a distance of some two hundred miles to Wantage, a small middle England village, and from there we boarded GMCs to the Farm, which was another six miles. Arriving just at daybreak, tired and hungry, we felt that this was the last straw as we gazed upon this forlorn array of buildings that had just recently been used to house horses. And they still hadn't been cleaned so well. This feeling of disgust ran through the whole battalion. The hearty breakfast of powdered eggs (our first) and Graham crackers didn't help any either. All that, combined with the smell of the stables, the heavy English fog, and the struggle we had with the packs and barracks bags didn't go to further the "good neighbor policy."

We were assigned to our "stables" immediately after breakfast and in a kind of daze we went about getting our belongings straightened out. How we would ever get used to this smell was a question in our minds. The best thing was to scrub them out with hot water and try to remove as much of the accumulated manure as possible. We started on this work at once.

All this work, together with that of doing Sergeant Bender's details and the classes to get us oriented to England and the customs of its natives, caused the weeks to pass swiftly. Soon we launched into an intensive training program. This was broken only by weekend and afternoon passes to Oxford and the villages in the vicinity of the Farm that was to become the second home of the 321st.

We gradually became accustomed to the kind of lingo used by the English and could now understand even the most exaggerated Oxford or Cockney accent. We were hardly aware of the change that we were going through. What had been "saloons" soon became "pubs." Beer was now spoken of as "mild and bitters." Your money was now definitely pounds, shillings, and pence. Common English phrases were soon picked up and used frequently by the Yanks, such as "Bloody well browned off," "You've had it," and "Get Cracking."

As your acquaintance with the natives grew, you learned that, though they had suffered and sacrificed a great deal during the war, they were still a friendly and tolerant people who possessed a sense of humor that you never fully understood but which you really appreciated. You began to look forward to the trips to Oxford with enthusiasm. The English girls were really impressed with the tall tales of America. Some of the guys certainly spread it on thick. These females soon picked up the Yanks' dances and such to make the fellows feel at home. Some of the families opened their doors to the boys from America who had traveled so far to help destroy the enemy that had set out to conquer the world. As a rule they all expressed their appreciation of the material help that come from the vast stores of the United States. Such opinions pleased you and made you feel very proud of your great country, especially when you took time to compare it to this little "fog infested" island of theirs.

There was a lot of work attached to this, however. The training program was of the hardest. Soon after it began we started to eat more food and to sleep more soundly. We did calisthenics and foot drill every day. We practiced the art of Jiu jitsu until all had sore arms and backs. Once a week we had a hike of any length between and inclusive of twelve to twenty-five miles.[1]

101st Airborne paratroopers from the 502nd Parachute Infantry Regiment in Normandy check out a crashed U.S. Waco glider on June 6. *Brothers in Arms: Road to Hill 30 screenshot*

As the air armada of C-47s approached the French coast, it encountered fog and antiaircraft fire, which forced many of the planes to break formation. Paratroopers missed their drop zones (DZs) and were scattered over wide areas. For many the first struggle of combat was to find their units. When small groups of paratroopers finally assembled, they had difficulty in identifying their locations relative to their objectives. The paratroopers of the 101st were promised reinforcements at dawn, when fifty-one of the division's gliders

Paratroopers under fire in Normandy on June 7. *Brothers in Arms: Road to Hill 30 screenshot*

JUNE 9, 1944, NORMANDY, 321ST GLIDER FIELD ARTILLERY BATTALION

At 2100 hours, June 9, we hit the beach and found the other group of our battalion waiting for us.

For the remainder of the evening that there was enough light, we de-waterproofed guns and vehicles. Our infantry was hurting for artillery support and we had to hurry. We had sent a forward observer [FO] to jump in with the 506th Parachutists. Their job was to direct naval and self-propelled 105 fire until we got in. This proved to be the only support the infantry had for the first few days, due to our being held up in getting ashore. The 377th Parachute Field Artillery, who had jumped in, succeeded in getting only one gun together and this was used mostly for direct fire. The 65th Armored F.A. [Field Artillery], veterans of the Mediterranean Theater, provided most of the artillery for the division during the first phases of the invasion, having come ashore at H plus 3 hours.

In the two days that followed, our FOs worked with the infantry, directing fire from a number of sources until we landed. In one instance they fired on a German troop concentration and when a count was taken there were 135 dead Krauts scattered around.

We came onto the beach amid a hail of bullets from two M.E. 109s [German fighter aircraft] strafing the area. Their action was short lived. A Spitfire was following them in and about one burst for each one made them fold up and tumble to earth like a couple of quail.

We moved inland about three hundred yards and began the de-waterproofing. The next morning just at daybreak we went into position near Pouppeville where we fired our first rounds against the Germans.

That night we were bombed and strafed. An ammo dump was hit nearby and as it began going off it gave us the impression that the whole German army was loose right under our noses. From this position we fired on Carentan until it was captured by our infantry. After this key town was taken we moved to a position near Katz, crossing the Douve River on a hastily constructed pontoon bridge. During this time we fired in general support of the infantry until the Germans were driven back a distance of three thousand yards. There our lines were secured and we took up a defensive position to allow supplies to be brought in for the drive to Cherbourg and at the same time to cut off the whole peninsula.

The 9th Division drove through to the west coast of Normandy while we were clearing Carentan. There they anchored their lines with parts of the division, using the rest to turn north and begin mopping up the Germans defending that end of the peninsula. As soon as Carentan was cleared, we moved again to strengthen our defensive position in order to keep the Germans from breaking through to their forces that had been cut off.

At this time the 79th and 90th divisions landed and moved inland to the main highway between Carentan and Cherbourg. With a whole division on either side of the highway they fought through to the high ground overlooking Cherbourg. In doing this, several small pockets of Krauts were sealed off in the vicinity of Valognes. These were cleaned up in short order after the fall of Cherbourg.

Having brought up strong reinforcements, the Germans made several vicious attempts to break through our lines to relieve their troops and at the same time to push us back into the sea. Every time they were beaten back with heavy losses to themselves.

We remained in this position for fourteen days. We were relieved by the 79th and then moved to another position southwest of St. Sauvier Le Compte, remaining there only one day. Again we moved. This time to a position near Cherbourg where we were put in reserve to guard the city and await transportation back to England. Sniper patrols were sent out daily. Other than that we did nothing but have inspections and get fined. Ever get caught without your helmet on?

During the Normandy campaign the battalion fired 11,850 rounds of 75mm ammo and spent 34 days in combat. [2]

Paratroopers form a hasty firing line in Normandy on June 7. *Brothers in Arms: Road to Hill 30 screenshot*

Corporal Joe E. Oleskiewicz, a member of the 506th Parachute Infantry Pathfinders known as the "Filthy Thirteen," is decked out in Mohawk war paint just prior to the Normandy invasion. *U.S. Army photo*

An M-5 Stuart tank from the 70th Tank Battalion supports 101st Airborne Division paratroopers in St. Côme du Mont on June 8. *Brothers in Arms: Road to Hill 30 screenshot*

were scheduled to land. The gliders, however, had problems of their own. Many of the gliders crashed, and several soldiers of the division were killed, including Brig. Gen. Don F. Pratt, the assistant division commander. A second glider landing at dusk that day produced even more casualties.

The men of the division, however, persevered and proceeded with their assigned missions as best they could. By nightfall soldiers from the 101st had secured the beach exits in their zone and contacted the landing forces of the 4th Division. The Screaming Eagles also controlled the La Barquette lock but could not secure crossings on the Douve River. The following day 101st elements attempted to advance in the division's southern sector but made little progress against heavy enemy resistance near the village of St. Côme du Mont. That same day General Eisenhower directed that American efforts be focused on closing the gap between the V and VII Corps. The VII Corps received orders to capture the town of Carentan, and the 101st, already in position outside St. Côme du Mont to the northwest, was given the task.

THE TEN COMMANDMENTS OF THE GERMAN FALLSCHIRMJÄGER (PARATROOPER)

1. You are the chosen ones of the German Army. You will seek combat and train yourselves to endure any manner of test. To you the battle shall be fulfillment.

2. Cultivate true comradeship, for by the aid of your comrades you will conquer or die.

3. Beware of talking. Be not corruptible. Men act while women chatter. Chatter may bring you to the grave.

4. Be calm and prudent, strong and resolute. Valor and enthusiasm of an offensive spirit will cause you to prevail in the attack.

5. The most precious thing in the presence of the foe is ammunition. He who shoots uselessly, merely to comfort himself, is a man of straw who merits not the title of Parachutist.

6. Never surrender. To you death or victory must be a point of honor.

7. You can triumph only if your weapons are good. See to it that you submit yourself to this law—first my weapon and then myself.

8. You must grasp the full purpose of every enterprise, so that if your leader be killed you can fulfill it.

9. Against an open foe fight with chivalry, but to a guerrilla extend no quarter.

10. Keep your eyes wide open. Tune yourself to the topmost pitch. Be nimble as a greyhound, as tough as leather, as hard as Krupp steel, and so you shall be the German warrior incarnate.

General Dwight D. Eisenhower gives the order "full victory or nothing else" to paratroopers of the 502nd Parachute Infantry Regiment, 101st Airborne Division, just before they board their aircraft at Greenham Common Airfield in England on the night of June 5, 1944. Eisenhower asked Pfc. Dan McBride of F Company, 502nd Parachute Infantry Regiment, "Are you scared?" McBride answered, "No, sir!" Eisenhower replied, "Well, I am!" amid gales of laughter from the nearby paratroopers. *U.S. Army photo*

Lieutenant Colonel Robert S. Wolverton (kneeling) of the 3rd Battalion, 506th Parachute Infantry Regiment, inspects the parachute harness of Capt. Stanley E. Morgan just before takeoff on June 5, 1944. Wolverton was killed by German troops in Normandy. *U.S. Army photo*

On June 8, elements of the 501st and 506th PIRs, along with the 1st Battalion, 401st GIR, engaged a German force in the town of St. Côme du Mont. The 3rd Battalion, 501st PIR, took positions south of the town, along the highway to Carentan where it encountered the enemy. The 1st Battalion, 401st GIR, was called to aid the 3rd Battalion, but the enemy withdrew before the glider troops arrived. Both of the 101st battalions pursued the retreating enemy, but there was no additional contact. The Germans had abandoned the town, and the Screaming Eagles moved in to plan the next step in the drive on Carentan.

The attack on Carentan was to be two pronged. The right arm of the drive was to cross the causeway northwest of Carentan, bypass the town, and continue to the southwest to occupy La Billonerie, also called Hill 30, which, it was thought, covered potential escape routes available to the Germans. The left arm of the assault was to cross the Douve River near Brevands, with the main body of that force continuing on to Carentan, while a smaller portion of the force moved east to the Vire River to contact the V Corps.

Paratroopers of the 101st Airborne Division advance as American P-47s attack German positions in Normandy outside Carentan, France. *Brothers in Arms: Road to Hill 30 screenshot*

The 3rd Battalion, 502nd PIR, led the right drive along the causeway. Progress, however, was extremely slow. In the dark, the men of the 502nd advanced along the causeway with no cover, facing steady fire as they moved forward. The battalion inched along until it reached the bridge on the Madeleine River and ran into a strong enemy position concentrated in an old farmhouse and the adjoining hedgerows. Lieutenant Colonel Robert G. Cole, the battalion commander, called for artillery fire on the position, but it did no good. Pinned down, as dawn broke, Cole's paratroopers flattened into the marshy swamp for cover. After unceasing enemy fire prevented any move for more than an hour,

A heavily laden Pathfinder team and the pilots who will deliver them to Normandy. Note the hastily painted invasion stripes on the fuselage of the C-47 aircraft. Tape has been applied to the door to ensure the edges do not cut the parachutes' static lines. *U.S. Army photo*

Troop carriers and gliders transporting the 325th Glider Infantry Regiment, 82nd Airborne Division, on June 6, 1944. This photo was taken from the cockpit of a WACO CG-4A glider and demonstrates the same method used to tow gliders of the 101st Airborne Division. *U.S. Army photo*

A Screaming Eagle outside Carentan after repulsing the counterattack of the 17th SS Panzergrenadier Division on June 13. A flight of American P-47s passes overhead. *Brothers in Arms: Road to Hill 30 screenshot*

Lieutenant Colonel Cole weighed his options. Withdrawal would mean returning across the same deadly causeway in broad daylight. Pinned down, he ordered a charge with fixed bayonets. Lieutenant Colonel Cole leapt up to lead the charge, but in the confusion of the fighting not all his men had gotten the word. The executive officer prodded the men along, and Cole continued with the soldiers who had followed. The Germans withdrew from the farmhouse, and the charging soldiers cleared the hedgerow positions.

Having suffered heavy casualties in the movement and the charge, the battalion was in no shape to pursue the withdrawing Germans. The 1st Battalion, 502nd PIR, which had also taken heavy casualties along the causeway, joined the 3rd Battalion to defend the newly taken position. The next morning when the Germans launched a strong counterattack, the battalions held their ground until they were finally

Screaming Eagles of the 101st Airborne Division pose with a captured Nazi flag in the village of St. Marcouf, France (near Utah Beach), on June 8, 1944.

U.S. Army photo

relieved by the 2nd Battalion. Elements of the 506th PIR relieved the beleaguered battalions of the 502nd on June 12. By that evening the 506th had completed the drive past Carentan and occupied Hill 30.

While the 502nd struggled along the causeway, the 327th GIR, with the battalion of the 401st, had led the left-wing attack. On June 10, elements of the force crossed the Douve River and occupied the town of Brevands. Company A, 401st GIR, continued southeast toward the town of Auville-sur-le-Vey to contact the V Corps, which had landed at Omaha Beach to the northeast. Encountering stiff German resistance outside the town, the company broke through the enemy line to make contact with the V Corps' 29th Infantry Division. The 327th, after crossing the Douve, had orders to seize both the railroad bridge and the highway bridge that crossed the Vire-Taute Canal, blocking the eastern escape routes from Carentan. The regiment succeeded in capturing and holding the highway bridge, but the railroad bridge was blown in the fight. The men of the 327th crossed the canal and continued their fight toward Carentan until enemy resistance halted their progress about a half mile from the town.

At General Taylor's direction, Brig. Gen. Anthony C. McAuliffe, commander of the 101st's artillery, coordinated the final drive for Carentan, which took place on June 12. Throughout the night of the 11th, the town was placed under heavy fire, but unknown to the U.S. forces, the main body of Germans, comprised primarily from the 6th *Fallschirmjäger* Regiment, withdrew under cover of darkness. The following morning the 2nd Battalion, 506th PIR, entered Carentan from the southwest and connected with the 1st Battalion, 401st GIR,

After D-Day some of the difficult fighting on Omaha Beach was attributed to the fact that U.S. paratroopers landed only behind Utah Beach and not Omaha Beach. The Americans suffered three thousand casualties on June 6, 1944, at Omaha Beach. *U.S. Army photo*

General Bernard L. Montgomery decorates Maj. Gen. Matthew Taylor, commanding general, 101st Airborne Division, with the British Distinguished Service Order on June 12, 1944. *U.S. Army photo (RG 208-PU-138KK)*

which approached from the northeast. Once the two battalions had linked up, they proceeded to clear the town of the remaining enemy stragglers. Under orders to secure the approaches to the town, the 501st and 506th moved along the roads to the southwest, while the 327th advanced to the east. Both groups, however, met enemy opposition, and their progress was limited. On June 13, the Germans launched a fierce counterattack in an attempt to retake the town.

The U.S. First Army directed elements of the 2nd Armored Division to support the 101st in defending Carentan. Together the riflemen of the 101st and the tanks of the 2nd Armored stopped the enemy thrust and threw the Germans back.

Two days later the 101st was reassigned to VII Corps. With the mission of establishing defensive positions across the Cotentin Peninsula, the VIII Corps gave the Screaming Eagles responsibility for securing the left flank of the VII Corps. On June 27, the 83rd Infantry Division arrived and relieved the 101st. Two days later the 101st was relieved from the VIII Corps and sent to Cherbourg to relieve the 4th Infantry Division.

Later, near Cherbourg, General Taylor stood on top of a captured pillbox and told his battle-hardened veterans, "You hit the ground running toward the enemy. You have proved the German soldier is no superman. You have beaten him on his own ground, and you can beat him on any ground." Field Marshal (then General) Bernard Law Montgomery pinned the British Distinguished Service Order on General Taylor's jacket. The 101st remained as a First Army reserve until mid-July, when it returned to England for rest and training.

Taylor had not just been exaggerating Allied success for morale; the three-month battle for Normandy, from June through August, had devastated German forces. By mid-August the Germans could field less than ten functioning divisions of moderate capability, down from a peak of fifty active divisions. Nearly a quarter of a million German troops had been killed or wounded, with more than two hundred thousand captured— altogether nearly half the total number involved in the protracted battle. Field Marshal Erwin Rommel saw the writing on the wall by July 15, two days before he was wounded. In a letter to Hitler, Rommel wrote, "Our losses are so high that the fighting strength of the divisions is sinking fast. . . . The force is fighting heroically everywhere, but the unequal combat is nearing its end. It is in my opinion necessary to draw the appropriate conclusions from this situation."

Some German generals were concerned that they could lose the war in Europe by the end of September. As of August 29, General Oberst Walter Model stated:

General Bernard L. Montgomery, commanding general, Allied ground forces in Normandy, is seen here with Lt. Gen. Omar Bradley, commanding general, 1st U.S. Army, as they study a situation map on June 20, 1944.

U.S. Army photo

> *The divisions which were taken back from Normandy across the Seine under extreme difficulties and hardest fighting are armed only with a few medium weapons, in general only carbines, etc. The supply and material replacement required is absolutely insufficient. . . . The panzer divisions, at present, each have five to ten tanks ready to be employed. In regard to artillery, only isolated guns are left with the infantry divisions and isolated troops with the panzer divisions.*

For its part in the Normandy battles, the 101st had suffered 868 killed, 2,303 wounded, and 665 missing or captured. The division spent the summer replacing equipment, training new soldiers, and waiting for its next mission. At about the same time, General Eisenhower called for a headquarters that would oversee the Allies' airborne troops. In August 1944, he established the First Allied Airborne Army, controlling elements of the American and British (and Polish) armies. The new army was put to the test in September 1944 during the Allied thrust in northern Europe: Operation Market Garden.

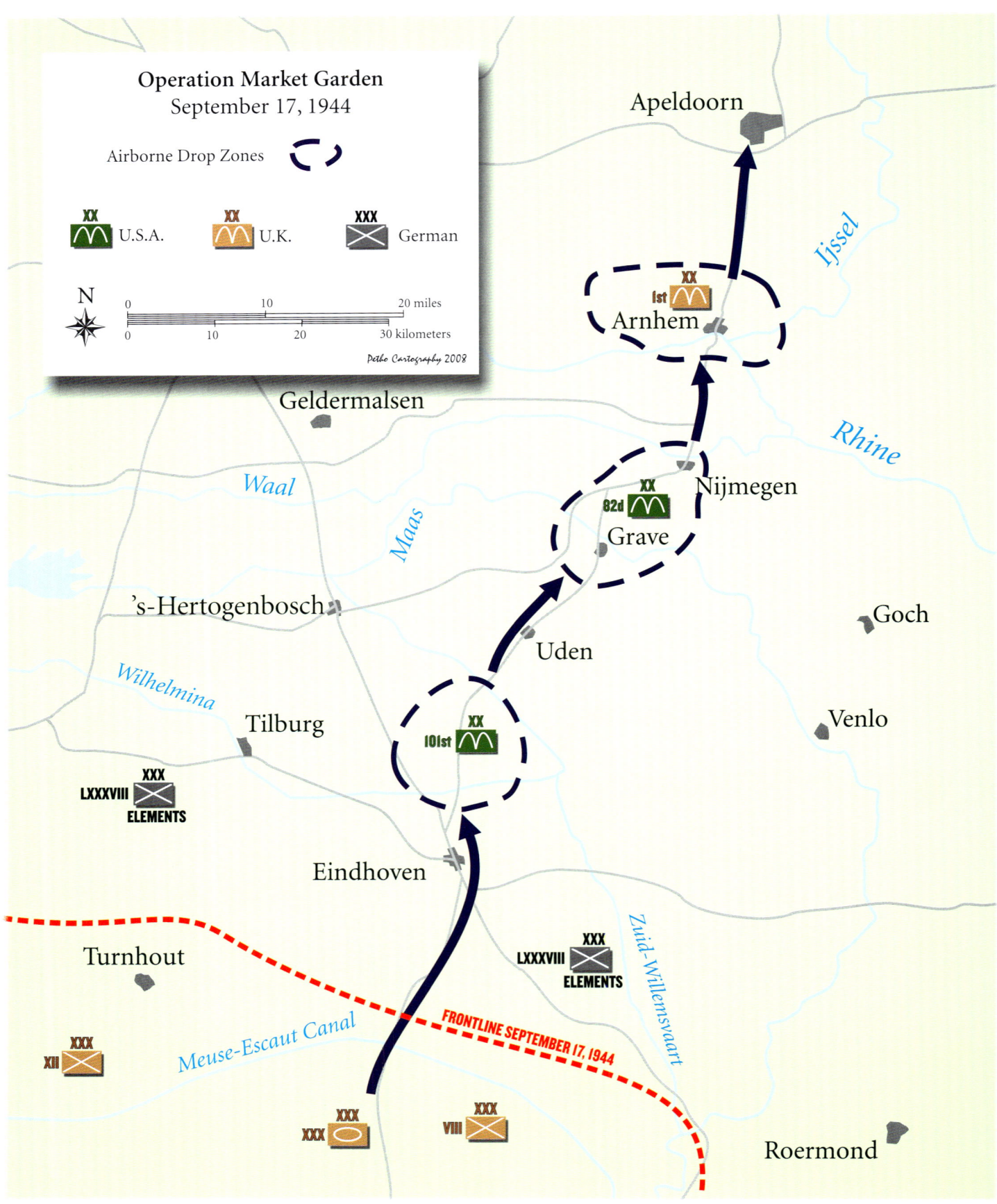

Operation Market Garden
September 17, 1944

Airborne Drop Zones

U.S.A. U.K. German

N

0   10   20 miles
0   10   20   30 kilometers

Petho Cartography 2008

Apeldoorn

Ijssel

Rhine

1st

Arnhem

Geldermalsen

Waal

Maas

82d

Nijmegen

Grave

Goch

Uden

's-Hertogenbosch

Venlo

Wilhelmina

101st

Tilburg

LXXXVIII
ELEMENTS

Eindhoven

Turnhout

LXXXVIII
ELEMENTS

Zuid-Willemsvaart

Meuse-Escaut Canal

FRONTLINE SEPTEMBER 17, 1944

XII

XXX VIII

Roermond

CHAPTER 3

Operation Market Garden

AFTER D-DAY, hard fighting had ensued in France in the hedgerow country around St. Lo and Caen, but when the eventual breakout from the Normandy beachhead occurred in late July, the Germans began to run, and the Allied operation turned into wholesale pursuit. Before the summer was over, the Allied armies, breaking out of their beachheads and overrunning France, appeared well on their way to accomplishing that goal. Meanwhile, the Russians, who had started their own big drive on the Eastern Front, advanced into eastern and central Europe. The giant Allied nutcracker was beginning to crush the German forces.

The essence of the plan of Operation Market was to use airborne forces to create a corridor [for the] main column. . . . The airborne corps was to drop near the key points all along this route, . . . overcome local resistance and dominate the bridges and highway intersections, and then hold until the Second British Army came through.

—101st Airborne Division, September 1944, Operation Market Report, dated October 10, 1944

German 88 destroyed in Normandy, France, on July 31, 1944.
U.S. Army photo

The Anglo-American armies link up to close the Falaise pocket. Lieutenant Harold Ashby of the British army exchanges information on the location of his parent unit with Maj. Harold Delp of the U.S. Army. *U.S. Army photo*

BY LATE SUMMER 1944, the German army was "no longer a cohesive force but a number of fugitive battle groups, disorganized and even demoralized, short of equipment and arms." In five years of war, the German military had suffered the death of 114,215 officers and 3,630,274 men. To the Allies, the horrific casualty figures of nearly 3 million men alone would prompt political upheaval within Germany or insurrection within the *Wehrmacht*. In July, an attempt was made on Hitler's life by a German officer. The attempt nearly succeeded.

With the Germans on the run, Allied commanders soon saw glittering opportunities at every turn. "These were the glorious days,

A destroyed German convoy in France, photographed on August 22, 1944. Although nearly one hundred thousand German troops escaped the Allies at the Falaise gap, they left behind between forty and fifty thousand prisoners and more than ten thousand dead. The roads were practically impassable with dead men, horses, and destroyed vehicles.

U.S. Army photo

FIRST ALLIED AIRBORNE ARMY

The interval of three months between Operations Neptune and Market, the next Airborne operation in the European theater, was marked by important organizational changes and by unprecedented fluctuations in the extent and character of troop carrier utilization. The principal change was the creation of the First Allied Airborne Army.

CHAIN OF COMMAND FOR OPERATION MARKET, 17 SEPTEMBER 1944
SUPREME HEADQUARTERS, ALLIED EXPEDITIONARY FORCE

ALLIED EXPEDITIONARY AIR FORCE

    SECOND TACTICAL AIR FORCE (BR)

    NINTH US AIR FORCE

US STRATEGIC AIR FORCES IN EUROPE

    EIGHTH US AIR FORCE

    SECOND BOMBARDMENT DIVISION

    14TH COMBAT WING+

    20TH COMBAT WING+

FIRST ALLIED AIRBORNE ARMY

    COMBINED TC COMMAND POST

    38 GROUP (BR)

    46 GROUP (BR)*

    IX TROOP CARRIER COMMAND (US)

    50TH TC WING

    52ND TC WING

    53RD TC WING

    IX TCC PATHFINDER GROUP (PROV)

FIRST ALLIED AIRBORNE ARMY (cont.)

HEADQUARTERS AIRBORNE CORPS (BR)

    FIRST AIRBORNE DIVISION (BR)

    52 DIVISION (AIRPORTABLE) (BR)

    82ND AIRBORNE DIVISION (US)

    101ST AIRBORNE DIVISION (US)

    FIRST POLISH PARACHUTE BRIGADE

    GLIDER PILOT REGIMENT (BR)

    MISCELLANEOUS SMALL UNITS

    XVIII CORPS (AIRBORNE) (US)

TWENTY-FIRST ARMY GROUP

    SECOND ARMY (BR)

    XII CORPS

    XXX CORPS

    GUARDS ARMORED DIVISION

    43 DIVISION

    VIII CORPS

*UNDER TEMPORARY OPERATIONAL CONTROL OF AIRBORNE ARMY FOR EMPLOYMENT IN MARKET

+BOMBER RESUPPLY MISSIONS IN MARKET COORDINATED WITH AIRBORNE ARMY C-3

The U.S. 28th Infantry Division parading in triumph after the battle on August 29, 1944. *U.S. Army photo*

the halcyon days of pursuit," wrote Charles B. MacDonald of the U.S. Army Office of the Chief of Military History. "The heartbreak of near stalemate among the hedgerows of Normandy . . . was past, an event belonging, it seemed, to yesteryear when the war still had to be won."

By August, Hitler's forces were defeated and raced back to the safety of their defenses in Holland and the Siegfried Line in Germany. Eisenhower was deeply satisfied with what the 101st Airborne and IX Troop Carrier Command crews had already accomplished and what they would do in the near future, telling them in an August 10 speech:

Any man in the world would feel honored to meet you. . . . But for your services the great operation proceeding in France perhaps could not have taken place. . . . I want to announce the First Allied Airborne Army . . . , for we have an opportunity to end this war far, far quicker than we could do without you. . . . The United States of the future is going to be deeply indebted to you. All the democracies will remember all your future and past exploits.

The Allies realized that a great opportunity existed to exploit the German defeat in France and end the war by Christmas 1944. "The August battles have done it and the enemy in the West has had it," stated a G-2 staff report from Supreme Headquarters, Allied Expeditionary Force (SHAEF). "Two and a half months of bitter fighting have brought the end of the war in Europe within sight, almost within reach." Airborne operations were often scrapped as ground troops advanced beyond the objectives of those plans. Yet the whirlwind advance also introduced complex logistical problems.

Still supported from the beaches at Normandy, and without an operational deep-water port in Allied hands, these supply lines were long and getting longer as the Allied armies marched toward Germany. With supplies of fuel and ammunition low, the forward movement slowed. Commanders juggled resources to keep the pursuit going. Even the Second Bombardment Wing of the Eighth Air Force was able to assist; although limited by the need for good, solid surfaces for landing, modified Liberators were able to fly nearly two thousand tons of freight from August 29 to September 17. By early September 1944, success was knocking at the door, but without a change in the broad front strategy that was established by General Eisenhower, something had to give. Some Allied generals believed that one strong push could bring about the collapse of Nazi Germany and the end of the war. Supply difficulties aside, this possibility seemed too good to pass up.

Lieutenant General Patton, Gen. Omar Bradley, and Field Marshall Bernard Montgomery (left to right) meet somewhere in France after D-Day to discuss the progress of the French campaign. *U.S. Army photo*

A Single Narrow Thrust

AS FIELD MARSHAL MONTGOMERY WAS ASKING for priority of supplies for a single thrust, Gen. George Patton was lobbying to be the one to lead the drive into the heart of Germany from the south. When Patton's Third Army ran out of fuel along the Meuse River, Patton blamed the British for getting the lion's share of the gasoline. Yet the British had their problems as well, despite the priority assigned them. A corps of the Second British Army, for example, was halted for two weeks west of the Seine so that its transport could help supply the rest of the army. A corps of the First Army also had to halt for four days in Belgium for want of gasoline.

At the end of August, the First Army estimated its daily average tonnage requirement as 5,500 tons. Even after General Eisenhower vested supply priority in the First Army and halted the Third Army, only 2,225 tons daily reached the First Army. In addition to immobilizing an entire corps for four days for want of gasoline, the First Army had to halt the armored divisions of the two advancing corps for periods as long as twenty-four hours.

Gasoline was the main problem, not because enough had not reached the Continent but because it could not be moved forward overnight and because worn-out vehicles used inordinate amounts. Ammunition presented no great problem during the mobile warfare of the pursuit, but it would, should a pitched battle develop at the gates of the West Wall. With all available transport used for daily maintenance and none for reserve stocks, what would happen should the armies run into intense fighting? How to equip the men with heavier clothing now that winter was coming on? How to replace the worn-out items of signal, quartermaster, medical, engineer, and ordnance equipment?

American light bomber struck by German flak during a low-level mission in Germany sometime in August 1944. *U.S. Army photo*

Paratroopers from the 82nd Airborne Division demonstrate how glider infantrymen sat inside a CG-4A Waco. There were a total of 1,051 troop carriers and 516 glider-tug combinations (2,083 aircraft in all) employed by the Allies on September 17, 1944, for Operation Market Garden.

U.S. Army photo

As many an Allied commander was to discover during the fall of 1944, a logistical headache is a persistent illness. Eisenhower realized that there were only two solutions: pause or capture new ports closer to the front. Meeting with generals Omar Bradley and Montgomery on August 23, General Eisenhower remarked that the supply situation would soon put the brakes to the Allied drive. The crux of the problem, as General Eisenhower saw it, was the lack of ports. To provide supplies for sustained operations into Germany, the Allies needed ports but, at this point, had only the Normandy beaches and Cherbourg. As a result, Eisenhower wondered if British Field Marshal Montgomery might reorient his drive to secure the port of Antwerp. In the process, Montgomery would also deny the Germans the use of the V-1 flying bomb launching sites, which had devastated London since June 1944.

Though Field Marshal Montgomery was interested in General Eisenhower's plan, he insisted on having an entire American army moving along his right flank. Because General Eisenhower already intended reinforcing the British with the airborne troops at his disposal, he thought Montgomery overcautious; but in order to ensure success, he acceded to the request, and the meeting resulted in a temporary shift of the main effort to the north.

Paratroopers from the 82nd Airborne Division practice tying down a 75mm howitzer inside a CG-4A Waco glider in preparation for air transport.

U.S. Army photo

The stage was set. Although a few dissenting voices tried to make themselves heard in the Allied camp, caution was not the fashion in early September 1944. Montgomery was confident that, with the Germans reeling, absolute Allied air superiority over western Europe, a powerful British armored corps primed and ready to strike, and a new Allied Airborne army ready to jump, he could bring a short end to the war. Montgomery came up with a daring two-phase plan, code-named Market Garden.

Operation Market was the airborne phase of the plan, calling for the First Allied Airborne Army—consisting of the U.S. 101st and 82nd

The Waco glider was vital to the Airborne for carrying heavy equipment—in this case, a jeep and four men. *U.S. Army photo*

Airborne divisions, the British 1st Airborne Division, and the free Polish Parachute Brigade—to drop into Holland. Landing in the vicinity of Eindhoven, Nijmegen, and Arnhem, these three-and-a-half airborne divisions would seize bridges over several canals and the Maas, Waal (Rhine), and Neder Rijn rivers. They were to open a corridor more than fifty miles long leading from Eindhoven northward and secure a narrow road that would become the axis of attack in the second phase of the plan.

Operation Garden had ground troops of the British Second Army attacking from the Dutch-Belgian border to the IJsselmeer (Zuider Zee), a total distance of ninety-nine miles. The main effort of the ground attack was to be made by the powerful British XXX Armoured Corps from a bridgehead across the Meuse-Escaut Canal a few miles south of Eindhoven on the Dutch-Belgian frontier. On either flank the British VIII and XII Corps were to launch supporting attacks.

Market Garden had two major objectives: crossing the Rhine and capturing the Ruhr. This would cut off the remaining German units in western Holland, outflank the West Wall, and position British ground forces for a subsequent drive into Germany along the North German Plain. The plan was bold, particularly with the strained logistical situation and the unpredictable nature of the weather in northwestern Europe in September.

While numerous signs pointed to the arrival of German reinforcements in Holland, the British believed these troops were few and of a "low category." Thinking back after the operation was over, the 1st British Airborne Division recalled, "It was thought the enemy must still be disorganized after his long and hasty retreat from south of the River Seine, and that though there might be numerous small bodies of enemy in the area, he would not be capable of organized resistance to any great extent."

General Bernard Montgomery was promoted to Field Marshal on September 1, 1944. His bold Market Garden plan would launch thirty thousand Allied airborne troops behind German lines with "thunderclap surprise" while British tanks and infantry drove up from Belgium along a narrow axis of attack and relieved the airborne troops. He believed the Allies could then thrust into the industrial Ruhr area and Berlin, ending the war by Christmas 1944. *British Ministry of Defense*

FROM THE DIARY OF TECHNICAL SERGEANT GEORGE KOSKIMAKI

SEPTEMBER 10, 1944

The news from the continent continues to be cheerful and the end of the European war is in sight. I doubt if us young punks will get to come home before Japan is knocked out of the war. We've heard all about the demobilization plan but we don't have a lot of men affected favorably by it.

SEPTEMBER 11, 1944

Twenty-four-hour passes were canceled again today and the war room is under strict guard. If we go to the marshalling area again, we'll go on a "wet run."

SEPTEMBER 14, 1944

Things are mighty hot for us again. We leave for the marshalling area. One office said this was positively a "wet run."

SEPTEMBER 15, 1944

I am getting all necessary data for the radio platoon. Learned we are going to help pave the way for the British Second Army. The mission is in Holland and our division is to capture and hold vital bridges.

SEPTEMBER 16, 1944

We were briefed today and received our foreign currency. Got our ammunition and made final check-ups on our weapons and parachutes. We are scheduled to land in Holland at 1330 tomorrow. I am jumping a fifty-pound radio leg pack. This will be different than Normandy where I jumped with only one-half of the present radio set. At the last minute I was bumped from General Taylor's plane. I suppose it is because I must jump in the number two position and there is danger I might hamper the drops of others in the plane. Brigadier General Gerald Higgins is jumping in the number three plane. General McAuliffe is coming in by glider on this one.

On September 10, General Eisenhower approved Market Garden, telling Field Marshal Montgomery, "I'll tell you what I'll do, Monty. I'll give you whatever you ask to get you over the Rhine because I want a bridgehead . . . but let's get over the Rhine first before we discuss anything else." A report from the Office of the Chief of Military History acknowledged that there was more than that behind Eisenhower's decision:

> General Eisenhower seems to have been influenced not only by a desire to get a bridgehead across the Rhine but by the hope of utilizing the First Allied Airborne Army, which had been awaiting action since July and August. Aware that Generals Marshall and Arnold were both deeply interested in the strategic use of airborne forces, General Eisenhower had sought a suitable occasion for employing these resources.

"The fact was that the paratroopers and glidermen resting and training in England had in effect become coins burning holes in SHAEF's pocket," said historian Charles B. MacDonald. "That is not to say that SHAEF intended to spend the airborne troops in a wild or extravagant fashion. Rather, SHAEF had decided to buy an airborne product and was shopping around."

> **The Dutch people were very supportive of our operations during Market Garden. In fact, the Dutch underground was a very valuable and dependable source of information. Overall, the Dutch were gracious, generous and grateful.**
>
> —*Pfc. Eduardo Peniche, 81st Airborne Antitank Antiaircraft Battalion, 101st Airborne Division*

On the same day as the approval of the plan, however, the British had remarked that "Dutch Resistance sources report that battered panzer formations have been sent to Holland to refit, and mention Eindhoven and Nijmegen as the reception areas." A few days later, Eisenhower's intelligence officer announced that these panzer formations were the 9th SS Panzer Division and presumably the 10th SS Panzer Division. They probably were to be reequipped with new tanks from a depot a few miles across the German frontier from Nijmegen and Arnhem.

Despite these warnings, the general view was that "once the crust of resistance in the front line had been broken, the German army would be unable to concentrate any other troops in sufficient strength to stop the breakthrough." Although the British XXX Corps would have to advance ninety-nine miles, leading units "might reach the Zuider Zee between two and five days after crossing the Belgian-Dutch frontier." They did have reasons for such optimism. British armored units had advanced seventy-five miles on September 3, taking Brussels on their way to Antwerp, which fell to them the next day.

The Germans in the West

ON SEPTEMBER 5, Hitler recalled Field Marshal von Rundstedt from retirement, put him in charge of the command of the Western Front, and placed Model in charge of Army Group B. Hitler told Rundstedt that the Allies were outrunning their supplies and soon would have to halt. When they halted, Hitler expected von Rundstedt to counterattack, cut

Field Marshal Gerd von Rundstedt was reappointed as *Wehrmacht* commander in chief of the west in early September 1944. He immediately worked to stabilize the German front. Highly respected by his troops, Rundstedt's steady leadership would turn the tide of German defeat in Holland. *U.S. Army photo*

The German army paid a terrible price in casualties and wrecked equipment during the retreat from France in the late summer of 1944, such as this burned out and abandoned Panther tank destroyed by Allied aircraft.

U.S. Army photo

This dejected German air cadet, placed in an infantry unit to stop the Allied advance, was captured by the U.S. Seventh Army near Villersexel, France, on September 13, 1944, four days before the launch of Operation Market Garden. The Germans were throwing every man into the line to stop the advancing Allies. *U.S. Army photo*

General Dwight D. Eisenhower, U.S. Army, nicknamed "Ike," was the supreme commander of the Allied forces in Europe and was charged with the overall planning and supervising the invasion of France and Germany in 1944–1945. Eisenhower was skeptical about Operation Market Garden, but when the Allied drive into Germany stalled due to insufficient supplies, Ike decided to keep the pressure on the Germans and gave Montgomery permission to launch the attack.

U.S. Army photo

off the "armored spearheads," and stabilize the front. The West Wall, Hitler insisted, could not be breached by the Allies and would gain time for von Runstedt to set up the conditions for such a success.

The force that von Rundstedt had to create this miracle was paltry. The retreating German troops possessed few heavy weapons and little else except carbines and rifles. Of the eleven remaining panzer divisions, few had more than five to ten tanks in working order. Artillery in both infantry and panzer divisions was nearly nonexistent. Morale was low. "Our own forces are tied up in battle, and in part severely mauled," von Rundstedt admitted. "They are short artillery and antitank weapons. Reserves worthy of mention are not available. The numerical superiority of the enemy's tanks to ours is incontestable. With Army Group B at the present time, there are some one hundred tanks available for action. The enemy air dominates the battle area and rear communications deep into the rearward terrain." Yet von Rundstedt was determined to stabilize the front and set about doing just that.

As German units retreated into Holland, they were collected and reorganized into kampfgruppes (ad hoc battle groups). Straggler rallying points were set up along the Albert Canal. Von Rundstedt gathered reinforcements from everywhere in his command. German parachute troops began to arrive in the army sector. Von Rundstedt's subordinate leaders worked wonders.

On September 3, the Fifth Panzer Army, retreating in disorder from France, had been ordered by General Model to release the 9th and 10th SS Panzer divisions to move to the vicinity of Arnhem for rehabilitation. Two days later Model ordered that headquarters of the II SS Panzer Corps under SS-Obergruppenfuehrer und General der Waffen-SS Willi Bittrich to the vicinity of Arnhem. General Bittrich was to direct rehabilitation of the 9th SS Panzer Division and two panzer divisions (the 2nd and 116th), which were to move to the Netherlands whenever they could disengage from combat.

While this movement was under way, Gen. Kurt Student, commander of the German First Parachute Army in Holland, threw in the bulk of his parachute troops against the British to stiffen German resistance noted along the Dutch-Belgian border. Student had assumed command of the western front's right wing on the Albert Canal as of September 4, stating, "At that moment I had only recruit and convalescent units and one coast-defense division from Holland. They were reinforced by a panzer detachment of merely twenty-five tanks and self-propelled guns."

On September 7, the 6th Fallschirmjäger Regiment arrived in the Netherlands and sent a battalion into Gheel to retake the town. While that action was "unexpectedly successful," as described by the regiment's commander, Oberstleutnant Friedrich-August Freiherr von der Heydte, other attacks in Belgium did not go so well:

[T]he main body of the regiment took part in an attack by the 85th Infantry Division—which consisted of only a divisional staff and its artillery regiment—against the bridgehead extending from Beeringen to across the Albert Canal, which was held by the British Guards Armored

321ST GLIDER FIELD ARTILLERY BATTALION, SEPTEMBER 16, 1944

On September 16, 1944, we were again alerted. Were we going this time? Was it just another dry run? What would our destination be if the departure became a reality? These were part of the many questions that were uppermost in our minds. Rumors flew thick and fast, flared up, became strong and died. None of us knew anything for sure. The army has a way of taking care of its vital secrets.

Then came the morning, the whistle. The day of going to the departure airfield had arrived. Everything was in readiness. Guns and Jeeps were on the line, seemingly eager to be on their way. A few goodbyes to heartbroken buddies. FO (forward observers) and liaison parties, and the 321 moved from Whatcombe Farm. It was a happy and adventurous crew that ruled the highways that Sept. morning. A twinkling eye for the pretty girls, a warning smile to the elderly. We were on our way and glad to be on the move.

Though we had experienced it many times, our first sight of the field with its rows upon rows of C-47s and gliders again brought to us the realization of the importance of our division. There they stood, winged power! And we were the men to make them so.

We were assigned to billets of pyramidal tents. Each section as closely associated with itself as possible. Clean new blankets, showers, entertainment, the best of food. Everything to make our last hours under normal conditions as enjoyable as possible.

But we still had work to do. Gliders had to be loaded and lashed. Loaded to fly and, if necessary, to crash land under the most adverse conditions. Arduous months of training had equipped us with the knowledge to do this job with the minimum of confusion and delay. Briefing, the job of telling what, where, and when to do a thing. The sand table now became our classroom. The position of every hedge, road, or river must be instilled in our minds. It was here that the question of where was answered with the naming of Holland as the destination.

All was in readiness now. Though a certain degree of "sweating it out" prevailed, the men as a whole were confident, sure of themselves and ready to go.

Volley[ball] and baseball teams were hastily organized. The Red Cross now became a gathering place. The food being excellent, many was the man who stood in line for seconds. Though no time had been set for "lights out," darkness usually found the men bedded down, clean healthful fun having retired them to a heavy sleep.[1]

Members of the 101st Airborne Division are issued hand grenades before loading into C-47 aircraft to parachute into Holland. *U.S. Army photo*

Joe's Bridge

Joe's Bridge is the name given to Bridge No. 9 on the Meuse-Escaut Canal (the Flemish name is Maas-Schelde Canal) in honor of the Irish Guards under the command of Lt. Col. J. O. E. Vandeleur. The bridge is located near the Belgian city of Lommel just south of the Belgian-Dutch border. At 2030 hours, the bridge was captured by British troops in September 10, 1944, when the Irish Guards rushed the German defenders, taking them completely by surprise and dismantling the demolition charges that the Germans had placed on the bridge before the Germans could detonate them. The Irish Guards lost only three men wounded in this action and gained a priceless crossing site for XXX Corps. Joe's Bridge became the jumping-off point for the British XXX Corps during Operation Market Garden.

The capture of the bridge was part of a larger operation to encircle German forces in the Hechtel area. For the next several days, the Germans tried to retake the bridge from the north but were forced back by the Irish Guards, who fiercely defended their prize crossing site across the Meuse-Escaut Canal. As soon as the bridge was secure, the engineers of the 615th Field Squadron, Royal Engineers, repaired it for crossing operations, and it became the start point for the British XXX Corps for Operation Market Garden on September 17, 1944.

Troops of the 231st Brigade cross Joe's Bridge on September 15, 1944, as the British XXX Corps continues to expand its bridgehead across the Meuse-Escaut Canal. *U.S. Army photo*

Division. No ground worth mentioning was gained. . . . [After being] transferred to the Postel-Luyksgestel area [the regiment] took part in an attack by the newly formed Divisiongruppe Walther, with its command post at Valkenswaard, on September 15 against the British bridgehead across the Maas-Schelde Canal. This attack, which was carried out entirely without artillery support, also failed.

In the meantime, the German Fifteenth Army, trapped on a peninsula in the west, began to ferry forces across the Schelde estuary. By September 16, some of these units, second echelon battalions, numerous other headquarters units, and several Luftwaffe battalions formed from Luftwaffe noncommissioned officer training schools were available to back up the German line.

Planning for Market Garden Continues

FIELD MARSHAL MONTGOMERY set the target date for the attack as September 17. This decision meant that the airborne troops and XXX Corps had but seven days to plan and prepare, but with the Germans on the run, it was vital to attack before they could turn the rout into a defense. With that in mind, Field Marshal Montgomery had made his decision on the side of speed.

Due to a series of planning factors involving available moonlight, enemy antiaircraft defenses, the number of available transport aircraft, and the problems of launching a night airborne operation, General Brereton decided that the airborne landings would be made in daylight and coordinated with the attack by XXX Corps.

Terrain was also a critical factor in the plan. Between Eindhoven and Arnhem, the highway that would become the attack route for XXX Corps passed through flat, open country crossed by canals and rivers.

It was all a question, therefore, of bridges. The bridges over the waterways along the route to Arnhem were the principal objectives of the three airborne divisions. Dropping in the south between Eindhoven and Veghel, the 101st Airborne Division was to secure approximately fifteen miles of the corridor, including the city of Eindhoven and bridges at Son, St. Oedenrode, and Veghel. The 82nd Airborne Division was to drop in the middle to capture bridges over the Maas at Grave, the Waal at Nijmegen, and the Maas-Waal Canal in between, plus the high ground southeast of Nijmegen. To the 1st British Airborne Division was given the prize, the bridge at Arnhem.

The start line for the main attack by the XXX Corps, under Lt. Gen. Brian G. Horrocks, was the bridgehead north of the Meuse-Escaut Canal, captured by Lt. Col. J. O. E. Vandeuleur's Irish Guards on September 10, 1944, thirteen miles below Eindhoven. By moving behind a heavy curtain of artillery fire and fighter bomber attacks, General Horrocks hoped to achieve a quick breakthrough with the Guards Armored Division, supported by the 43rd and 50th Infantry Divisions.

General Horrocks assigned the armor a D-Day objective of the village of Valkenswaard, six miles short of Eindhoven, where XXX Corps would make contact with the 101st Airborne Division. Yet General Horrocks said informally that he hoped to be in Eindhoven within a few hours—before nightfall—on D-Day and expected to reach Arnhem "before the end of D+3." Over this highway to Arnhem, he told a briefing conference, he intended to pass twenty thousand vehicles in sixty hours.

The goal was to get to Arnhem as rapidly as possible. The Dutch countryside, criss-crossed by innumerable dikes, drainage ditches, rivers, and canals, however, would prove difficult to traverse if the ground troops could not advance by road. For the plan to be a success, the paratroopers had to keep the roadway open and the bridges along the route intact and secure.

Two 101st Airborne paratroopers from the 502nd Parachute Infantry Regiment. *Brothers in Arms: Road to Hill 30 screenshot*

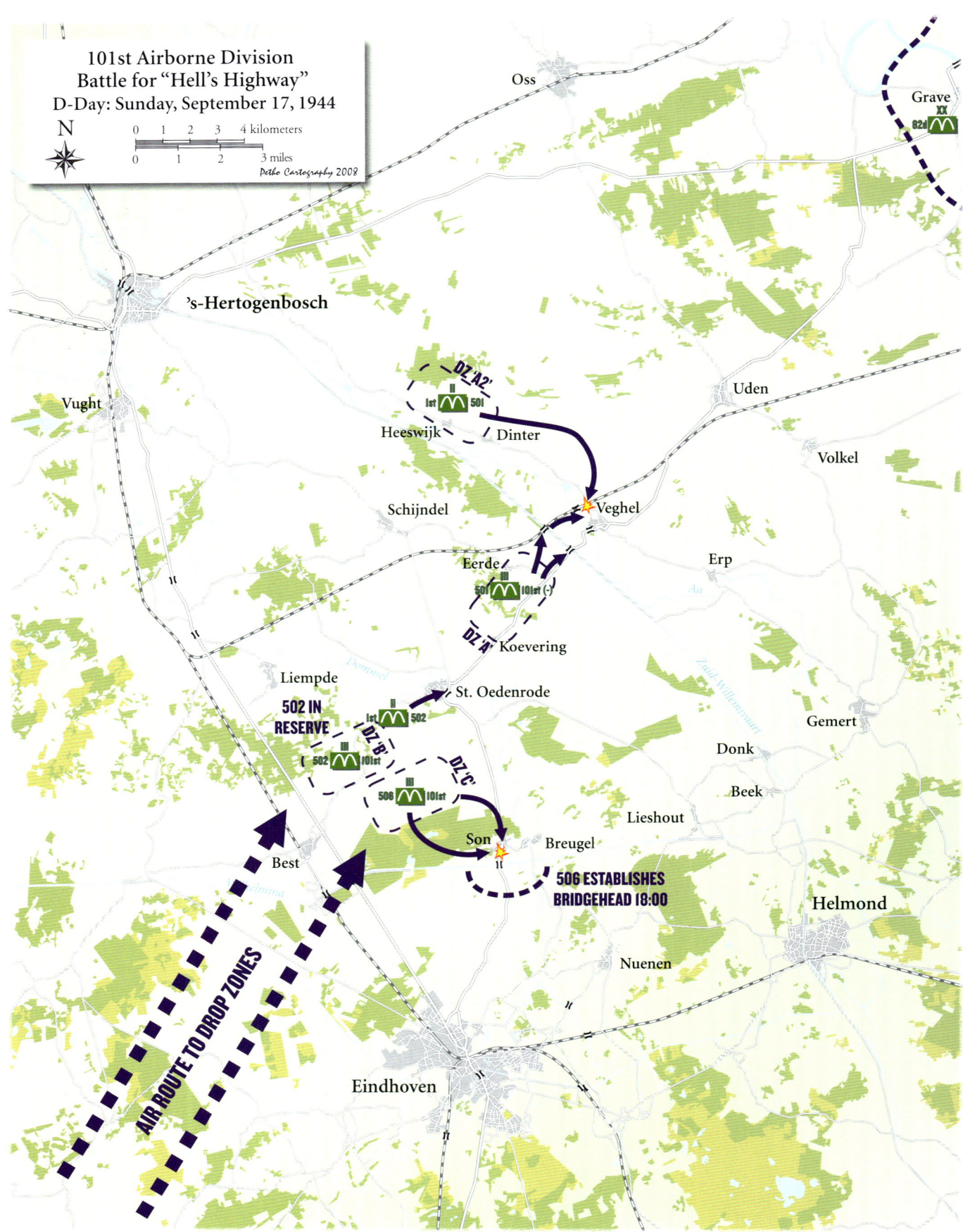

101st Airborne Division
Battle for "Hell's Highway"
D-Day: Sunday, September 17, 1944

N

0 1 2 3 4 kilometers

0 1 2 3 miles

Petho Cartography 2008

Oss

Grave
XX
82d

Vught

's-Hertogenbosch

DZ 'A2'

1st 501

Heeswijk   Dinter

Uden

Volkel

Schijndel   Veghel

Eerde   Erp

501 101st (-)

DZ 'A'

Koevering

Aa

Liempde   St. Oedenrode

Gemert

502 IN
RESERVE

1st 502

Donk

DZ 'B'

502 101st

Beek

DZ 'C'

Lieshout

506 101st

Best   Son   Breugel

Helmond

506 ESTABLISHES
BRIDGEHEAD 18:00

Nuenen

AIR ROUTE TO DROP ZONES

Eindhoven

CHAPTER 4

D-Day: September 17, 1944

OPERATION MARKET GARDEN started before dawn on September 17, 1944, with more than 1,400 bombers attacking the German troops between Eindhoven and Arnhem. At 0900, around the time the air raid sirens went off in Arhnem, Lieutenant General Horrocks called Colonel Renfro into his tent to review the 101st Airborne's mission. After quickly covering their drop zones, landing zones, and objectives, Horrocks peppered Renfro with additional questions about rations and other supplies. Renfro then realized that Horrocks shared Renfro's own skepticism about Market Garden. When Horrocks and Brigadier General Pyman, Horrocks' chief of staff, asked Renfro for his thoughts on the plan, he answered, somewhat noncommittally, "It's all right." Horrocks' response was laughter.

Now every man is out. . . . I can see their chutes going down now. . . . They're dropping beside the little windmill near a church, hanging there, very gracefully, and seem to be completely relaxed, like nothing so much as khaki dolls hanging beneath green lampshades. . . . The whole sky is filled with parachutes?

—Edward R. Murrow in one of the 101st Airborne's C-47s recording for CBS Radio, September 17, 1944

C-47s on their way to Holland on September 17, 1944. *U.S. Army photo*

THE PLANES CARRYING THE 101ST started taking off in the morning. As they flew over Holland, the aircraft encountered heavy antiaircraft fire, but the pilots held formation and the paratroopers, for the most part, were delivered to the correct drop zones. Nearly seven thousand Screaming Eagles parachuted down toward the drop zones located to the west of the main highway and in the center of the division's sector, near the villages of Son, St. Oedenrode, and Best.

According to General Student, it had been "a remarkably beautiful late summer day. All was quiet at the front. Late in the morning, the enemy air force suddenly became very active. . . . From my command post at Vaught, I was able to observe numerous enemy aircraft; I could hear the crash of bombs and fire from aircraft armaments and antiaircraft guns in my immediate vicinity. . . . At noon there came the endless stream of enemy transport and cargo planes, as far as the eye could see." Hitler's reaction was immediate. At a September 17 operations conference at his Wolfschanze (Wolf's Lair) headquarters in East Prussia, he raged, "Holland overshadows everything else!" He then gave top priority to reinforcements and Luftwaffe support to stop the Allied drive into Holland. Although the Germans had been expecting an air attack, they assumed the Allied forces would strike at night. Surprise was complete, and the 101st Airborne Division landings were virtually unopposed.

LT. GEN. BRIAN HORROCKS, COMMANDER, XXX CORPS: THE BEGINNING OF THE ATTACK INTO HOLLAND

I heard on the wireless that the Airborne divisions were on their way. Suddenly, the armada appeared overhead. Hundreds of transport planes in perfect formation, many towing gliders, droned steadily northward, protected on all sides by fighters. . . . It was a comforting thought that some thirty thousand Airborne troops were being dropped or landed from gliders in front of us.

As soon as the air armada came into view, I ordered "Zero hour 1435 hours." At 2:00 p.m. (1400 hours) precisely, there was a sudden deafening roar and a noise as though an express train were passing overhead. Our guns had opened up their counter-artillery program, and the battle of Arnhem was on. Under the cover of the preliminary artillery bombardment, the Irish Guards started moving into position just short of the start line.

At 2:35 p.m. (1435 hours) exactly, Lt. Keith Heathcote of No. 3 Squadron 2nd Battalion Irish Guards—a tank regiment—ordered "Driver advance" and one of the greatest breakouts in history had started. A hundred yards in front of Heathcote's tank rolled a curtain of fire [from] some 350 guns. In front of this again was an endless stream of R.A.F. Typhoon fighters pouring their rockets into the German defenses. From my command post the whole battlefield was visible, and for the first ten minutes all seemed to be going well. But just when we were congratulating ourselves that our blasting tactics had proved successful, the whole situation changed. . . . Within two minutes the Irish Guards had lost nine tanks, and the whole advance was held up by accurate fire from enemy antitank guns.

I could not help a fleeting feeling of admiration for the fighting qualities of the Germans, for in spite of a terrific battering, both from the ground and the air, they were still fighting stubbornly.

The 502nd Parachute Infantry Regiment hitting their drop zone near Son, Netherlands, on September 17, 1944.

U.S. Army photo

Only fifty-three of the seventy gliders carrying the 101st's heavy equipment (jeeps, antitank weapons, and supplies) landed safely, however. "On the outside of our CG4A Waco glider someone had chalked the prayer: 'I hope to God the crew of this glider land safely,' to which I mentally added my name," recalled Cpl. H. Spence, I British Airborne Corps Signals, who was attached to the 101st Airborne during Market Garden.

Of course, the C-47s were no guarantee of safety; a number of them caught fire as they took enemy flak. Several pilots saved their paratroopers and got them to the drop zones by staying at the controls

There Goes the Wing!

The serial in which Sink (Col. Robert Sink, commander, 506th PIR) and Chase (Lt. Col. C. H. Chase) were traveling began getting light flak about ten minutes out. Five minutes out, it struck with tremendous volume against the column coming along on their immediate left in the forty-plane formation. Many of the ships were hit, and the men who were in the ships of the CO (commanding officer, Colonel Sink) and his exec (executive officer) could plainly see the damage. Chase, who was in Plane No. 2, was watching for the green light and looking at Plane No. 3 as they came on in. He figured they were two minutes out and he told the stick to stand up. At that moment he saw No. 3 blazing fiercely from the left engine. No. 3 kept going, neither losing altitude nor changing its course. Then he forgot No. 3, for looking at his wing, he saw a hole come through it—quite suddenly. He looked for the green light, looked back again—now two feet of the wing had been sheared away. Then the green light flashed. Colonel Sink, who was in Plane No. 1, had been looking out of the door. Something shook the body of the plane and he saw a part of the wing whip off and dangle in the breeze. He turned and said: "Well, there goes the wing."[1]

Landing by glider was one of the most dangerous ways for airborne soldiers to get to the battlefield. This glider collided with another in mid-air over the drop zone at Son. The glider carried a Jeep and three men from the 501st Parachute Infantry Regiment. Members of the 506th Parachute Infantry Regiment dug out the survivors from the wreckage.

U.S. Army photo

Two disabled CG-4A Waco gliders near the landing zone outside Son.

Brothers in Arms: Road to Hill 30 screenshot

while their planes burned around them. Lieutenant Colonel Hank Hanna of the 101st told this story:

> *When we passed over the British Second Army and into hostile territory, the flak commenced raining on us from Eindhoven. My plane was hit in the left engine and left tail section and some of it came through the floor at the front of the plane where no one was seated. The fire became so intense that the motor cut out and we had to jump prematurely. However, the pilot held on so tenaciously that we were able to jump within a mile of the DZ. The crew chief jumped out after we had gone. I saw him in Son*

American paratroopers regroup in the drop zone as C-47s continue dropping more troops. *Brothers in Arms: Road to Hill 30 screenshot*

later, but the plane went down in flames. I have not learned about the pilot, copilot, and navigator, but I'm afraid they didn't make it—perhaps because they stuck it out for us.

The 506th PIR dropped near Son, with the mission of securing the bridge over the Wilhelmina Canal, south of the village. Once the bridge was secure, the regiment was to advance farther south and seize Eindhoven. The 502nd's zone was north of the 506th, and its mission was to guard both regiments' drop zones for later use by the gliders. It was also to capture the road bridge over the Dommel River at St. Oedenrode. Additionally, General Taylor ordered the regiment to dispatch a company to the south of Best to capture the bridges there that crossed the Wilhelmina Canal. The

A squad of Screaming Eagles takes up a hasty firing line in this reenactment photo. The helmet markings of these paratroopers designate them as members of the 1st Battalion, 502nd Parachute Infantry Regiment, also called the "Five-Oh-Deuce."

Author photo

Paratroopers of the 501st Parachute Infantry Regiment pass by a windmill as they enter the town of Eerde. Dutch civilians on bicycles are there to greet and assist the American liberators. Today, a small monument to the 501st is located near the mill, and the mill itself bears plaques memorializing fallen members of the 501st and the British 44th Royal Tank Regiment, as well as the citizens of Eerde who perished in the fighting. *U.S. Army photo*

501st PIR jumped north of the 502nd, near the village of Eerde. Elements of the regiment were to gain control of the rail and road bridges over the Willems Canal to the northeast, then proceed to take the town of Veghel and the rail bridge over the Aa River north of the town.

The 501st accomplished its mission, seizing Veghel and the four bridges against only limited enemy resistance. Although 2nd Lt. Robert P. O'Connell remembered the capture occurring "quite quickly," it was still a deadly battle. "In working along a street fight in Veghel, we killed three Krauts and, as we moved up the street, I jumped over their bodies and thought—30 seconds ago they were alive. The reality of the war came to me then."

When we went into Son . . . we received ovations, cheers, offers of food, smiles, and an acceptance so whole-hearted and unrestrained—so unlike our reception in Normandy—that it nearly brought tears to my eyes.

—Lt. Col. Hank Hanna, 101st Airborne Division

The 502nd also completed its main assignment of securing St. Oedenrode and the bridge over the Dommel River. The company that had moved south of Best, however, had great difficulty and could not take the bridges over the Wilhelmina Canal. The 2nd and

D-DAY, SEPTEMBER 17, 1944

The 506th Parachute Infantry landed on DZ C without enemy opposition. Companies of the 1st Battalion departed immediately without formal assembly in an effort to secure the three bridges over the Wilhelmina Canal in the vicinity of Son before they could be blown up by the enemy. Scattered enemy resistance was encountered before reaching the main bridge and forward elements were within 100 yards of this bridge when it was blown by the retreating enemy. (It was found that the other two bridges had been blown several days before.) The regiment began the crossing of the canal by various expedients and by 2400 the entire regiment was on the north side of the canal and had a bridgehead extending some 2,000 yards.

The command echelon of division headquarters jumped with the 502nd Parachute Regiment and established an initial command post at Son. Some 70 gliders carrying additional command personnel, the reconnaissance platoon, signal and medical personnel, and some transportation for the combat units, landed on the LZ about one hour after the parachute landings. Overall time of landing of all parachutists and gliders was one and a half hours. Communications were established with all elements except the 501st by dark on this date.[2]

3rd battalions, 506th PIR, methodically cleared Son, while the 1st Battalion, accompanied by General Taylor, moved around the village to the south to seize the bridge crossing the Wilhelmina Canal at that location. The canal bridges were crucial for the Allies' advancement; the sixty-foot-wide canals were too deep for tanks to drive across. The rivers, none of which were wider than twenty-five feet, did not present as imposing an obstacle.

Taylor, with division objectives stretched out along the highway for more than fifteen miles, had brought his forces in midway between

Immediately following their landing behind German lines in Holland, American paratroopers disperse to begin taking their initial objectives in the vicinity of Son, Netherlands.

U.S. Army photo

Diary of Technical Sergeant George Koskimaki

I'm writing from a slit trench in our first assembly area. We jumped at 1327 after going through considerable flak. Quite a few planes were knocked down. Our company lost five of fifteen gliders. It was far more exciting than the first in France. I "sweated out" this one a lot more than the first one. Our first jump occurred at 0126 on the morning of June 6. This one came at approximately 1330 in the afternoon of Sunday, September 17.

The night before the jump, I did all my sweating and praying. I did not sleep well at all. I kept waking with nightmares of myself going down tangled in my lines; my chute failing to open; and the plane being shot down. I was one of three men jumping a "leg bag" containing a radio set. The total weight of this lad was just over fifty pounds. This pack was attached to my leg when I climbed into the plane. A guy can't walk with it without lifting that pack and foot with his two hands. The way it does work is that the jumper throws his heavily weighted foot out of the door and is himself dragged out by its weight and the force of the prop wash striking the bag.

Again it was our opportunity to be the first American troops in an airborne invasion—and this one into Holland. We were working with the British this time.

There was a heavy fog on the ground Sunday morning and we even had ideas of a postponement, but the general came around and said weather forecasts had a clear sky over the continent and the fog in England would lift before takeoff time.

We marched out to the planes past long lines of Air Corps ground personnel who I imagine were mighty glad not to be in our boots. I kind of wished I were in the Air Corps at the time, but I couldn't be away from my buddies. Our plane had no name. It had never been on a parachute drop mission. We were introduced to the crew by the jumpmaster (Master Sgt. Connie Russell of our Wire Platoon). The pilot built up our morale. He was just a little guy but he gave us a very heartening pep talk.

The takeoff was much like the one on our first D-Day. It was an impressive sight to watch the planes behind us take off two at a time. Air Corps personnel stood on both sides of the runway waving as each plane roared by into the air.

This was our first chance to really get a good look at England from the air. It was a beautiful sight in the

Long lines of C-47 transport planes are loaded with men and equipment at an airfield in England. The C-47s carried the Screaming Eagles of the 101st Airborne Division to Holland to launch Operation Market. *U.S. Army photo*

bright sunlight. I don't imagine I can write about cities we pass over because it would give away the route of flight. Looking out the door (I was sitting beside it) one could see an endless chain of planes in perfect formation as far as the eye could see.

It was cold up there even at two thousand feet. We flew across the Channel and I watched the shadows of the planes in their formation on an almost placid sea. Air-Sea rescue craft were everywhere just in case a plane ran into trouble.

We picked up our fighter escort at mid-Channel. It was above and below and to either side of us. We crossed into Belgium. We got our first bird's-eye view of the effects of Allied bombing as we passed over leveled factory buildings.

The landscape in Belgium was pretty with large green fields cut by small canals. Now and then we'd pass one of the large canals such as the Albert Canal, which was rimmed with tall Lombardy Poplar trees. People could be seen below pedaling along on their bicycles.

The front was rapidly approaching as we neared the Dutch border. The lines were separated by bright panels to show strafing pilots which troops were friend and foe. The snapping, such as was heard in France, started. It was enemy small-arms fire. I looked down and saw one C-47 burning on the ground. How its occupants made it out, I do not know.

We were over heavy flak for about fifteen minutes. I was second man this time because of the cumbersome load I was carrying. We stood up—four minutes out from the "DZ" (drop zone). The plane bounced as a sister plane was hit and caught fire. The pilot of that plane brought his load over the DZ and dropped them safely before bailing out himself. Cattle and chickens were scurrying everywhere, disturbed by the terrific bombardment coming up at us.

I stood with the heavy leg in the doorway just behind the jumpmaster. He shouted, "Let's Go!" and out we went. My chute opened with that pleasant jerk that almost tore my shoulders loose. It meant my chute was open. The radio bag was ripped loose from my gloved grasp by the shock and now dangled on the toe of my boot. My folding stock carbine had been ripped loose from its canvas holster and hung loosely, attached to me only by its front sight, which was caught in the untorn portion of the holster.

I tried to draw my right foot up so I could release the radio equipment bundle but fifty pounds was too much to draw to a suitable height. With my left foot, I finally managed to push the bundle off the toe of the boot, and then pulled the little ripcord that enabled the bundle to drop about thirty feet below me where it dangled like a pendulum still attached to my parachute harness. I didn't have to guide my chute as I was headed

C-47s towing CG-4A Waco gliders of the 1st Allied Airborne Army on the way to Holland. *U.S. Army photo*

for a large plowed field. I hit the loosely tilled soil and made the softest landing I have ever experienced.

I became aware of crashing and thumping sounds about me and noted the sky was filled with rifles, helmets, equipment packs, and other items which had not been secured well. These parted company with their owners and now had to be avoided like rain.

We jumped near a small town, and the Germans took off on all available transportation after first blowing a bridge that went a hundred yards into the air before coming down in little pieces.

continued on page 58

Unlike the nighttime drop of June 6 in Normandy, the daylight drop in Holland enabled C-47 pilots to get most of the Screaming Eagles to their designated drop zones. This accurate drop allowed General Taylor's men to quickly assemble and move out to their assigned objectives. *U.S. Army photo*

As we left the field, people ran out to us with milk and sandwiches. Each of us was thumped on the back and had our poor hands almost rung off by handshakes. One thing they don't do is kiss like the French people. It made some of the boys down-hearted because there were pretty girls here also.

All of the people had orange bands of cloth on their left arm to show they were still fighting Dutchmen. They helped us in a hundred different ways, such as aiding men with broken bones resulting from the jump, taking horses and carts, and hauling our extra equipment off the field for us. People lined the streets handing out apples, peaches, pears, and tomatoes to the boys as they passed by. It makes a guy feel mighty proud to fight when it is appreciated like it has been thus far.

Our first night was very quiet due to the fact that our landing had a discouraging effect on the Germans. A counterattack would come, but not today. One important thing I forgot to mention was the Typhoons and P-38 Lightnings strafing and dive bombing flak towers and antiaircraft emplacements. They did a wonderful job of it. I saw one such place flattened to the ground, yet a Dutch farmhouse thirty yards away was untouched.

Paratroopers move off the drop zone in this reenactment photo. The lead soldier is carrying an M1 Garand rifle. The soldier behind him carries an M1919A4 .30-caliber Browning light machine gun, while the man behind him carries the tripod. The .30-caliber Browning was a critical weapon for the American Airborne infantry. *Courtesy of Brian Perkins*

This bridge at Son (open to allow boats through) was a vital crossing point along Hell's Highway and a critical objective of the 101st Airborne Division. Unfortunately for the Americans, the Germans had prepared the bridge for demolition and then blew up the bridge on September 17 just as the American paratroopers tried to capture it. *NARA photo*

Son and St. Oedenrode. The idea was to be able to quickly attack both villages on the way to Eindhoven. The progress of the battalions in Son was slow, however, and enemy fire stopped the 1st Battalion completely as it approached the bridge. As the 2nd and 3rd battalions finally emerged from Son and the 1st Battalion also appeared to advance, the Germans blew the bridge:

The battalion began getting casualties—about ten men altogether being wounded at this stage. Rifle, machine-gun, bazooka, and finally mortar fire were placed on the house. The battalion drew closer to the canal as it concentrated on this last obstacle. The house became silent. The leading group of all three rifle companies had drawn to within thirty to fifty yards of the banks, and the first men from 1st Battalion, 506 PIR, had come up to their right flank. Colonel Sink was about seventy yards to their rear. And then the bridge went up with a roar. Debris fell down all around the upcoming infantrymen, already stunned by the surprise of the blast.[3]

Elements of the 506th managed to cross the river, neutralizing the enemy force that had destroyed the bridge, and a footbridge was improvised to allow the remainder of the 506th to cross.

A German machine gun fires from a steeple in Son as an American paratrooper ducks for cover. *Brothers in Arms: Road to Hill 30 screenshot*

The paratrooper returns fire with his M1 Garand. General Patton called the M1 rifle "the greatest battle implement ever devised." *Brothers in Arms: Road to Hill 30 screenshot*

At about this same time, German soldiers near Vaught found a crashed glider containing a copy of the entire Operation Market Garden plan, including the locations of landing zones and a detailed time schedule. The plans were quickly sent up the German chain of command, and soon General Student had a copy on his desk:

> Though surprised by the airborne force and not prepared for an attack, General Student was able to draw on the II SS Panzer Corps, then regrouping northeast of Arnhem, and to bring up to Nijmegen the II Parachute Corps with several parachute Kampfgruppen, which were reorganizing near Cologne. Student was aided by a captured copy of the Allied attack order, which reached him within two hours after the landing. An infantry division, en route to the area from the Fifteenth Army area at the time of the attack, was detrained and put into the attack against the 101st Airborne Division near Son. The enemy was also helped by the fact that Field Marshal Model, who had his Army Group B headquarters near Arnhem, was able to coordinate the fighting at Arnhem and Nijmegen. The defense was quickly organized and new forces brought up. The enemy sent all available combat aircraft to help his antiaircraft stop the Allied attack.[4]

The bridge at Son is blown up just as American paratroopers arrive. *Brothers in Arms: Road to Hill 30 screenshot*

A thirty-minute 350-gun artillery barrage preceded the

British infantrymen move up along Hell's Highway on September 17, 1944. Up ahead about one kilometer is the battle with German forces delaying the British push toward Eindhoven.

NARA photo

XXX Corps advance. At 1435 hours, the tanks from Lt. Col. J. O. E. Vandeleur's Irish Guards advanced as the artillery barrage began "walking fire" ahead of the lead tanks. Within minutes the lead tanks were hit by German antitank fire. Vandeleur called for air support, and a wave of Typhoon ground-attack aircraft plastered the German positions with rockets and bombs. German antitank units dug in on both sides of the road were cleared with tanks and infantry from the Irish Guards. After a sharp fight, the Irish Guards broke through the initial crust of the defense and headed toward Valkenswaard. They reached the town before dark when it was decided to stop for the night. Market Garden was already behind schedule. Colonel Renfro would report that "the quick 'ride into the blue,' which had been expected did not materialize."

American paratroopers from the 506th Parachute Infantry Regiment are assisted in locating the position of nearby German forces by eager Dutch civilians near the Merks family farmhouse near Son, Netherlands, on September 17, 1944. *U.S. Army photo*

THE FIRST DAY:
AN OPERATIONAL ASSESSMENT
OF OPERATION MARKET GARDEN

Despite prompt and unexpectedly strong enemy reaction, the Allies made some gains during the first day. By midnight, the 101st and the 82d Airborne divisions were well established near Eindhoven and Nijmegen. The 1st British Airborne Division, dropping some six to eight miles west of Arnhem, lost the effect of the initial surprise by landing too far from the objective. Elements of the division took the north end of the Arnhem highway bridge, which was still intact. Many miles to the south, British armored units, starting their advance in the early afternoon from the Meuse-Escaut Canal bridgehead, ran into heavy opposition from parachute and SS panzer troops. Even though progress was "disappointingly slow," the general feeling was one of optimism.[5]

321ST GLIDER FIELD ARTILLERY BATTALION ON SEPTEMBER 17, 1944

On the morning of the 17th at the hour of 1020 a tenseness filled the camp. Coming from the northwest could be seen hundreds of transports and gliders and we knew that our paratroopers and division artillery were on their way. They circled the field, jockeyed for position, and flew on, due east. We waved and wished them the best. We had confidence in them; they were our friends.

We knew that a large part of the initial success depended on them. With eager ears we awaited the news broadcast heralding their progress. It wasn't long in coming. "Allied parachute and glider troops have invaded Holland." They were there and the mission was under way. In about six hours the drone of engines told of the return of the carriers. We counted them. Yes, some were missing. That was to be expected. Then came the red flares denoting that some of the planes had injured persons aboard. That, too, was expected. We gathered around the pilots and copilots. What was it like? Was there much flak? This was the trend of the dozens of questions shot at the men

A special B-17 Flying Fortress from the 534th Squadron, 381st Bomb Group, carrying photographers and Gen. Matthew Ridgway, the commander of the U.S. XVIII Airborne Corps, to observe the airborne landings in Holland. *U.S. Army photo*

who had been there. On the morning of the 19th we were awakened by the throaty roar of the mighty transports as they warmed up prior to taxiing onto the runways. This was the day, this was IT.

Men tumbled from their bunks and hastily began preparation for leaving the area. A thorough check of the quarters was made by the officers and after a hearty breakfast we made our way to the waiting gliders.

There were naturally a lot of last minute details to be taken care of between the troops and pilots. These were handled in the usual Air Corps manner and at 1235 the first glider took the air. At 45-second intervals one glider after another rolled from the line. The 321st was Airborne. What was before us, only God in his Heaven knew.

Over the greens of England flew the Armada. As far as the eye could see stretched the chain of fighting men. Below us we could see the coast line, the channel with its treacherous currents and now Belgium.

Flying in close formation the ships encountered heavy fog banks. Visibility was so reduced that at the time only the first few feet of the tow line could be seen. Tug ships changed their course without the glider knowing it. Some of them were flopped over and had to cut loose. Then came the flak and heavy machine-gun fire. We could see the black smoke and dirt and knew that we were nearing the landing zone. We felt naked up there, knowing that thousands of faces, both friendly and enemy, were upturned to see us pass. With the spit of a thousand devils the fire surrounded us. Through the tail assembly, the floor, the very men themselves it penetrated. Ships and gliders went down but the huge formation never faltered.

Then we hit the earth. Alighting from our ferries, the sky seemed full and literally alive with gliders. Some bumped into those that were already landed. Others sheared their wings at the field's edge. Two of them even ran together head on, in midair.

But we were on the ground, and glad we were. Fifty-seven of the seventy-one gliders reached the LZ. Three howitzer loads came down in the channel and eleven were forced down in Belgium and Holland. Three of the tow ships were shot down in flames. Freedom is expensive.

The enemy had the western edge of the LZ zeroed in with mortar and small-arms fire and any gliders landing in that area were immediately brought under it. In spite of the difficulties encountered, we assembled quickly by 1640 hours. At 1845 hours we were in position and ready to fire.

FO parties were sent to direct fire in support of the 502nd Parachute Infantry as well as the 327th Glider Infantry. The 502nd was attacking Best and the 327th was holding Son.

All day long we could see the C-47s dropping in supplies. Those pilots certainly took a lot of punishment, from flak, from lack of sleep and rest.

Many of the planes were shot down, and since it was not always possible to recognize our troops, part of these supplies naturally fell into enemy territory. But enough planes did get through and delivered the goods.[6]

The Son drop zone strewn with CG-4A Waco gliders. The glider at the lower left has over-turned. *U.S. Army photo*

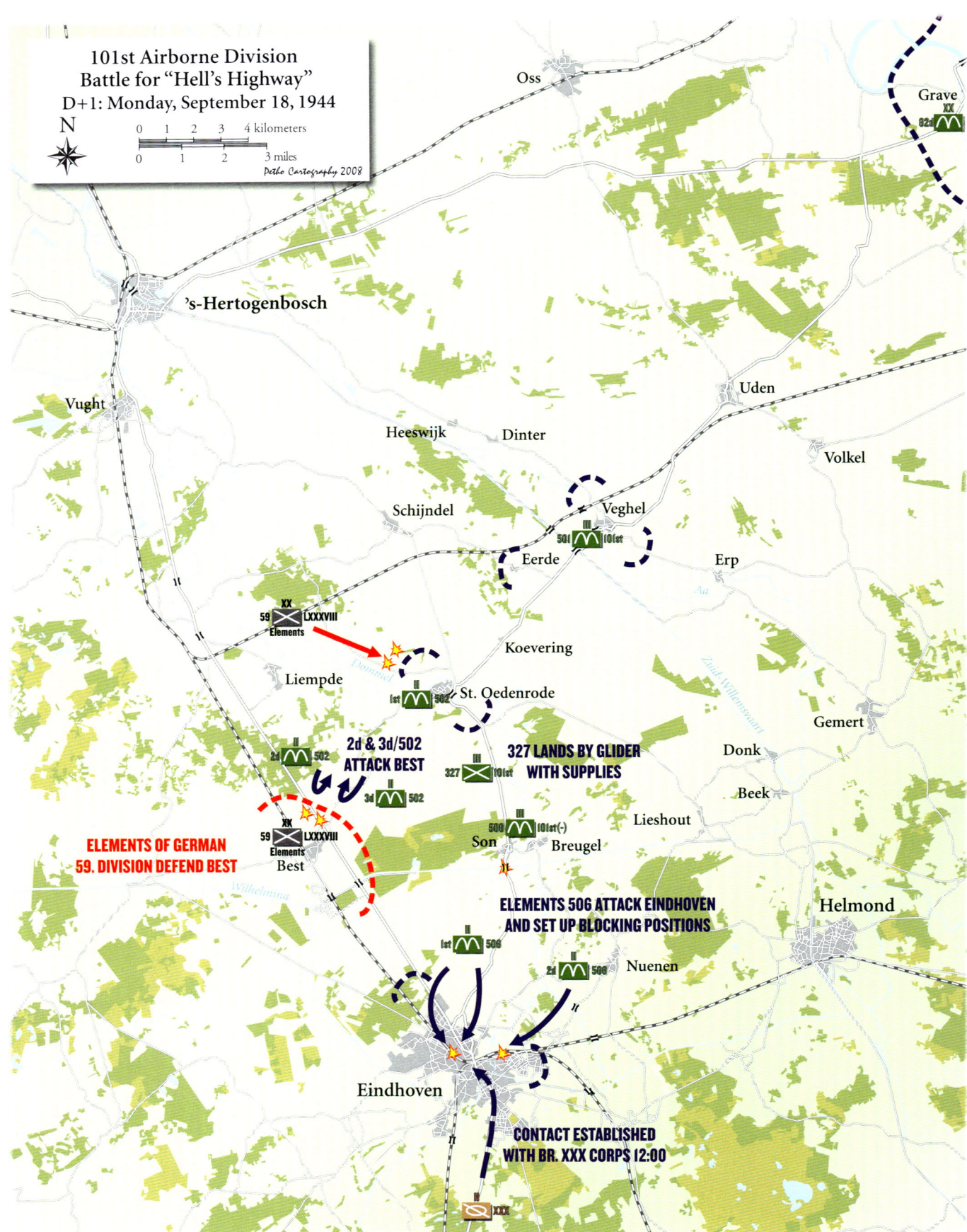

101st Airborne Division
Battle for "Hell's Highway"
D+1: Monday, September 18, 1944

N

0 1 2 3 4 kilometers

0 1 2 3 miles

Petho Cartography 2008

Oss

Grave

's-Hertogenbosch

Vught

Heeswijk

Dinter

Uden

Volkel

Schijndel

Veghel

Eerde

Erp

Koevering

Liempde

St. Oedenrode

Gemert

2d & 3d/502 ATTACK BEST

327 LANDS BY GLIDER WITH SUPPLIES

Donk

Beek

Lieshout

ELEMENTS OF GERMAN 59. DIVISION DEFEND BEST

Son

Breugel

Best

Helmond

ELEMENTS 506 ATTACK EINDHOVEN AND SET UP BLOCKING POSITIONS

Nuenen

CONTACT ESTABLISHED WITH BR. XXX CORPS 12:00

Eindhoven

CHAPTER 5

D+1: Monday, September 18

THE 501ST PIR CONTINUED the defense of Veghel throughout the day. Communication was established with division at 0600. Several light enemy attacks were repulsed, but no major effort to retrieve the town was made. The 1st Battalion, 502nd PIR, continued to hold St. Oedenrode and likewise repelled several light enemy attacks. The 3rd Battalion, 502nd PIR, attacked at first light in an effort to retrieve the highway bridge at Best but suffered heavy casualties at the hands of the enemy force, which had been strongly reinforced during the night. The 2nd Battalion was then ordered by Colonel Michaelis to assist the 3rd Battalion in securing the bridges; the loss of the Wilhelmina Canal bridge had intensified the 502nd's mission to secure alternates.

Captain John W. Kiley, battalion S-3 [operations officer], was killed by a sniper operating in the church tower. A bazooka rocket hit the tower and silenced the sniper, but the damage had been done.

—Recorded by Marshall and Westover in 101st Airborne Division, September 1944, Operation Market Report, dated October 10, 1944

Private Bernard M. Nakla, from Seattle, Washington, 101st Airborne Division, gives a stick of gum to a little Dutch girl after landing behind German lines. *U.S. Army photo*

SILVER STAR CITATION,
1ST LT. JOSEPH C. MACGREGOR

The Silver Star was awarded to Lieutenant MacGregor, 501st PIR, for an action in Veghel on the morning of September 18. MacGregor would later be killed in action in the defense of Hell's Highway, and the Silver Star was awarded posthumously. The citation read, in part:

> [T]he overwhelming superiority of the enemy greatly taxed the strength of his platoon and Lt. MacGregor was ordered to withdraw his men. Realizing that a critical situation had developed and the rapid withdrawal was imperative, Lt. MacGregor remained at the center of the road junction fully exposed to enemy fire and directed the movement of his confused forces. Desperately shouting orders to his men, he held back the onrushing enemy by firing his submachine gun from his exposed position, killing several of the enemy. This afforded his men sufficient time to effect an orderly and safe withdrawal. Although seriously wounded, he remained to direct his troops until the position was overrun, and he became, temporarily, a prisoner. He was rescued the following day by counterattacking, friendly forces. . . .

Paratroopers from the 101st Airborne Division move toward Eindhoven on the morning of September 18.

Brothers in Arms: Road to Hill 30 screenshot

THE BATTALION PENETRATED to the outskirts of Best but was forced to withdraw by heavy artillery, mortar, and small-arms fire and took up a defensive position to the left of the 3rd Battalion. At dark the entire regiment less the 1st Battalion was in a defensive position east of the highway facing the enemy defenses around the Highway Bridge at Best.

Aerial photo of Eindhoven. The 506th Parachute Infantry Regiment of the 101st Airborne Division battled remnants of German forces and captured the town before the arrival of the British XXX Corps.

U.S. Army photo

> **Now get your gang together and we'll start moving to that big town up there and then we'll take it. If any Germans try to come through us during our move up, let them go through and I figure Five-oh-Deuce [502nd PIR] will take care of them. We got to get that town and we won't waste time killing Germans.**
>
> *—Col. Robert Sink, Commander, 506th PIR, as his regiment was preparing to advance on Eindhoven, from the 101st Airborne Division, September 1944*[1]

At first light the 506th PIR, 3rd Battalion leading, moved on Eindhoven. A mile north of the city, at Woensel, determined enemy resistance stalled the 3rd Battalion. The 2nd Battalion outflanked the enemy defenses to the east of the city, seizing the town at 1300. At 1215 contact had been made with a British Reconnaissance Patrol north of Eindhoven. Sergeant Jack Maclean, part of a bazooka team of 101st U.S. Airborne Division was on the outskirts of Eindhoven when he heard the call for "Bazookas up front." They joined a platoon from

The Irish Guards Regiment from the British XXX Corps arrived in Eindhoven to cheering crowds on the afternoon of September 18. One soldier on this tank is opening a bottle of champagne that was given to him by an exuberant Dutchman. *NARA photo*

Company H in a flanking move that soon encountered some German riflemen and machine-gun emplacements. "The platoon drove them off and we were able to catch one 88 being backed into an alley," Maclean remembered. "We put three rounds into it, destroying it and killing the crew." By nightfall the regiment controlled the entire city and had taken up defensive positions around their main objectives, the essential bridges. The Guards Armored Column came across the bridges

A Dutch girl waves the Stars and Stripes in welcome as riflemen of the 327th Glider Infantry Regiment, 101st Airborne Division, march down the Eindhoven to Nijmegen road and a Jeep from Headquarters and Service Company rolls by. *U.S. Army photo*

from the south at 1850. The 506th's initial mission was complete.

The destruction of the bridge and the loss of time in getting [the] regiment across the canal weighed on Sink heavily. He felt that it might critically affect the whole operation and foredoom to failure the attack of the Second British Army. . . . He was still lacking the [news] that Second British Army (XXX Corps) was already stalled far below Eindhoven.[2]

Meanwhile, the operation continued back in England. By noon some 428 gliders—carrying the 3rd Battalion, 327th GIR, the engineer battalion, the remainder of the medical and signal companies, elements of the 377th Parachute Field Artillery (PFA) Battalion, and additional supply and administrative vehicles—were towed into the skies from English airdromes and headed for Holland. Casualties were suffered over the west coast of Holland from antiaircraft and machine-gun fire.

At about 1500 they reached their landing zones, touching down with light opposition. Of the 160 gliders of the 327th, 147 reached their goals with few injuries. Of the 13 that did not, 5 had landed back in England, 2 were missing, 3 went down in the English Channel, 2 landed nearly ten miles from the landing zone (LZ), and 1 crashed at the LZ with the loss of all personnel. Arriving at the combat area at about 1530, the 3rd Battalion, 327th GIR, was assigned the mission of providing local protection for the LZ and the division service area.

Brigadier General Anthony McAuliffe (left) with Colonel Whitacre, pilot of the C-47 that would tow McAuliffe's glider. McAuliffe flew in a glider to raise the morale of his men. Walter Cronkite, UP correspondent, flew in the same glider. *U.S. Army photo*

Brigadier General Anthony McAuliffe, the assistant division commander, 101st Airborne Division, briefs C-47 and glider pilots before taking off from England to reinforce the 101st on September 18, 1944. *U.S. Army photo*

MEDAL OF HONOR CITATION, PFC. JOE E. MANN

U.S. Army photo

Rank and Organization: Private First Class, U.S. Army, Company H, 502d Parachute Infantry, 101st Airborne Division. Place and Date: Best, Holland, 18 September 1944. Entered Service at: Seattle, Wash. Birth: Rearden, Wash. G.O. No.: 73, 30 August 1945.

Citation: He distinguished himself by conspicuous gallantry above and beyond the call of duty. On 18 September 1944, in the vicinity of Best, Holland, his platoon, attempting to seize the bridge across the Wilhelmina Canal, was surrounded and isolated by an enemy force greatly superior in personnel and firepower. Acting as lead scout, Pfc. Mann boldly crept to within rocket-launcher range of an enemy artillery position and, in the face of heavy enemy fire, destroyed an 88mm gun and an ammunition dump. Completely disregarding the great danger involved, he remained in his exposed position, and, with his M-1 rifle, killed the enemy one by one until he was wounded 4 times. Taken to a covered position, he insisted on returning to a forward position to stand guard during the night. On the following morning the enemy launched a concerted attack and advanced to within a few yards of the position, throwing hand grenades as they approached. One of these landed within a few feet of Pfc. Mann. Unable to raise his arms, which were bandaged to his body, he yelled "grenade" and threw his body over the grenade, and as it exploded, died. His outstanding gallantry above and beyond the call of duty and his magnificent conduct were an everlasting inspiration to his comrades for whom he gave his life.

MEDAL OF HONOR CITATION, LT. COL. ROBERT G. COLE

Rank and organization: Lieutenant Colonel, U.S. Army, 101st Airborne Division. Place and date: Near Carentan, France, 11 June 1944. Entered service at: San Antonio, Tex. Birth: Fort Sam Houston, Tex. G.O. No.: 79, 4 October 1944.

Citation: For gallantry and intrepidity at the risk of his own life, above and beyond the call of duty on 11 June 1944, in France. Lt. Col. Cole was personally leading his battalion in forcing the last 4 bridges on the road to Carentan when his entire unit was suddenly pinned to the ground by intense and withering enemy rifle, machine gun, mortar, and artillery fire placed upon them from well-prepared and heavily fortified positions within 150 yards of the foremost elements. After the devastating and unceasing enemy fire had for over 1 hour prevented any move and inflicted numerous casualties, Lt. Col. Cole, observing this almost hopeless situation, courageously issued orders to assault the enemy positions with fixed bayonets. With utter disregard for his own safety and completely ignoring the enemy fire, he rose to his feet in front of his battalion and with drawn pistol shouted to his men to follow him in the assault. Catching up a fallen man's rifle and bayonet, he charged on and led the remnants of his

U.S. Army photo

battalion across the bullet-swept open ground and into the enemy position. His heroic and valiant action in so inspiring his men resulted in the complete establishment of our bridgehead across the Douve River. The cool fearlessness, personal bravery, and outstanding leadership displayed by Lt. Col. Cole reflect great credit upon himself and are worthy of the highest praise in the military service.

C-47 transport planes tow gliders loaded with airborne troops and equipment on their way to Holland. *U.S. Army photo*

Waco gliders are lined up on an English airfield in preparation for the next lift to Holland. The 101st Airborne Division was reinforced with twelve glider serials on September 18. *U.S. Army photo*

THE LUFTWAFFE COUNTERATTACKS

On the 18th the Allied fighters had to contend with the first strong effort made by the Germans to intercept an Allied airborne mission. This effort was made in accordance with decisions taken by Hitler at a conference on the night of the 17th. The Nazi dictator had decided that since ground reserves were inadequate for a large-scale counterattack, the Luftwaffe would have to make an all out effort to tip the scales against Market. The German airmen were met on D plus 1 by the 357th and 359th Fighter Groups. The 359th Group, patrolling the perimeter with 57 planes, fought and repelled 35 FW-190s about 15 miles northeast of Arnhem, shooting down three of them and losing two of its own aircraft. The 357th Group, which was supposed to cover the Eindhoven area, was vectored out onto the perimeter about 40 miles southeast of Eindhoven to meet an attack. There, at 1505, while troop carrier operations were at their height, its 52 planes battled about 60 enemy fighters. The pilots claimed 26 of the Germans destroyed at a cost of two of their own planes. None of the Nazis got through to strike at the troop carrier columns that day.[3]

The Screaming Eagles prepare to take out a German FlaK 36, an 88mm cannon. "FlaK" is a German contraction of either "Flugzeugabwehr-Kanone" or "Flugabwehr-Kanone" (hence the capital K, nowadays one word) meaning anti-aircraft gun, the original purpose of the eighty-eight. *Brothers in Arms: Road to Hill 30 screenshot*

A resupply mission for later in the day did not have the same success rate:

> *The bomber resupply mission to the 82nd and 101st Divisions was to arrive 20 minutes after the troop carriers, drop time being set for 1557. It was to be flown by 252 B-24s of the 2nd Bombardment Division from bases in Norfolk and Suffolk. Supplies were trucked in on the night of the 17th. The ball turrets were removed, and each plane was loaded in bomb racks, waist, and bomb bay with about two tons of supplies packed in 20 containers. . . . After most of the briefing was done, it was discovered that the 2nd Bombardment Division had sent 20th Wing data to the 14th Wing and vice-versa. Since the correct maps and photographs were flown in just as the planes were warming up, pilots and navigators had to familiarize themselves with their route as they went along. . . . The results were not good. Even the wing commander admitted that the bundles were badly scattered. Some 238 tons were dropped. On DZ W, where 108 of the Liberators were to drop, only about 20 percent of the supplies were recovered.[4]*

Despite the setbacks, British forces reached the south side of the canal at Son at approximately 2100 and immediately began the construction of Bailey Bridge across the canal.

This glider had a rough landing near Son, but the crew—and their Jeep named "Ruth"— survived the landing. Jeeps provided a critical means of mobility for the 101st Airborne Division, especially for reconnaissance, artillery, and medical units. *U.S. Army photo*

A paratrooper from the 101st Airborne Division Reconnaissance Platoon prepares to engage the Germans. *Brothers in Arms: Road to Hill 30 screenshot*

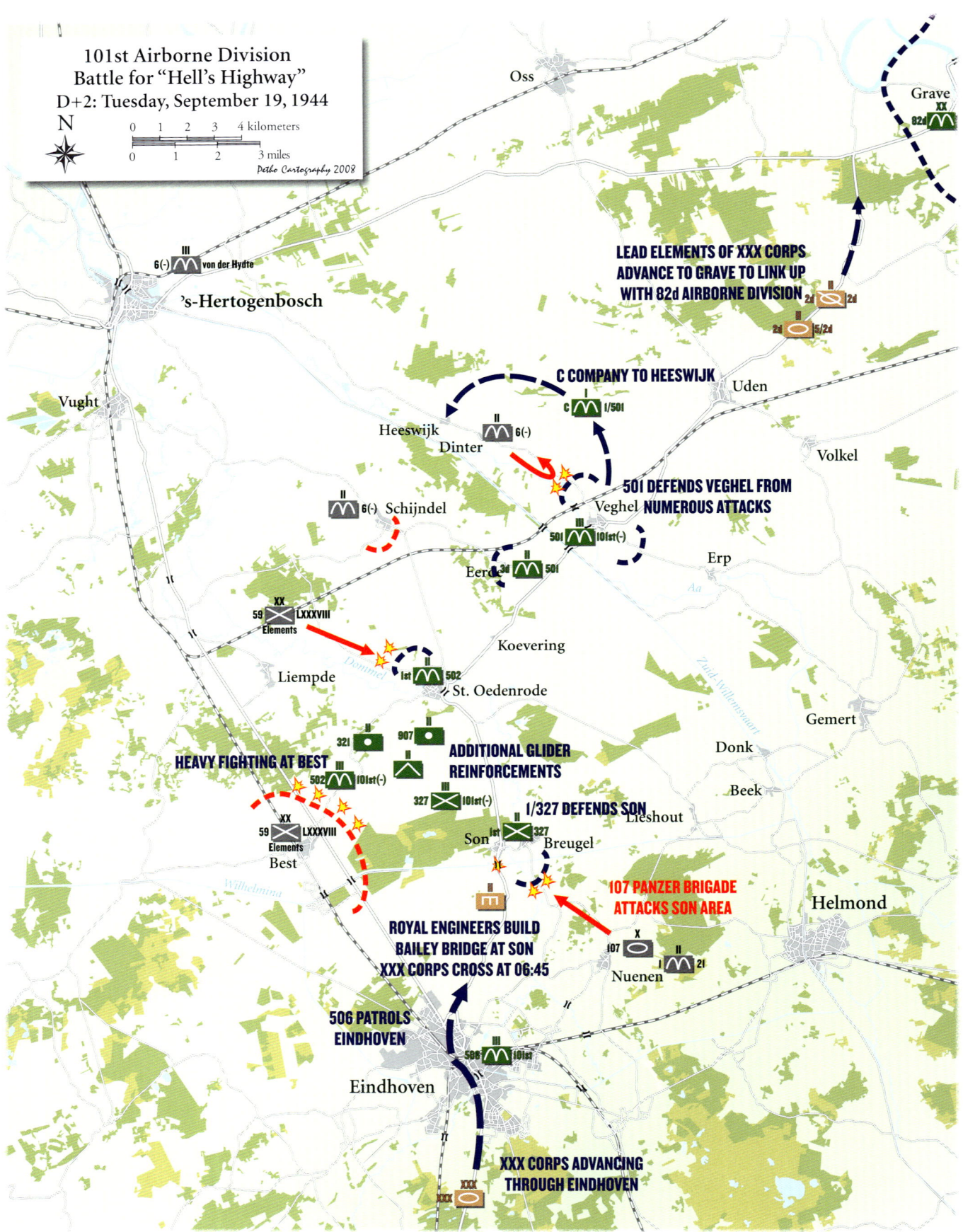

101st Airborne Division
Battle for "Hell's Highway"
D+2: Tuesday, September 19, 1944

N

0   1   2   3   4 kilometers
0   1   2   3 miles

Petho Cartography 2008

Oss

Grave

**LEAD ELEMENTS OF XXX CORPS
ADVANCE TO GRAVE TO LINK UP
WITH 82d AIRBORNE DIVISION**

's-Hertogenbosch

von der Hydte

Vught

C COMPANY TO HEESWIJK

Heeswijk

Uden

Dinter

Volkel

Schijndel

**501 DEFENDS VEGHEL FROM
NUMEROUS ATTACKS**

Veghel

Eerde

Erp

Liempde

Koevering

St. Oedenrode

Gemert

**ADDITIONAL GLIDER
REINFORCEMENTS**

Donk

HEAVY FIGHTING AT BEST

Beek

I/327 DEFENDS SON

Lieshout

Son

Breugel

**107 PANZER BRIGADE
ATTACKS SON AREA**

Best

Helmond

**ROYAL ENGINEERS BUILD
BAILEY BRIDGE AT SON
XXX CORPS CROSS AT 06:45**

Nuenen

**506 PATROLS
EINDHOVEN**

Eindhoven

**XXX CORPS ADVANCING
THROUGH EINDHOVEN**

CHAPTER 6

D+2: Tuesday, September 19

THE BRIDGE ACROSS THE CANAL was completed during the night, and at 0615 leading elements of the Household Cavalry and Guards Armored Division began crossing. These same leading elements passed through St. Oedenrode and Veghel by 0645. One squadron of the 15/19 Hussars was attached to the 506th at Eindhoven, and one squadron to the 502nd PIR at Son. Although ground forces continued forward, XXX Corps was now more than thirty-three hours behind schedule; recon troops of the Guards Armored Division, leading the corps' ground column, met the 504th PIR, 82nd Airborne Division, at 0820 in Grave.

During battle every commander must try to keep his subordinate commanders informed regarding the progress of the fighting. If it is impossible for him to give the broad picture, he must at least inform them regarding the progress of his own unit. In turn, subordinate commanders will pass this information along to their men.

—Notes on Leadership by Hans-Jürgen von Arnim, commander of Army Group Africa from March to May 1943. Arnim was captured in Tunisia in May 1943.

The light tanks of XXX Corps reached the bridge at the village of Veghel at 0645 on September 19, 1944. As this Sherman Firefly tank of the Grenadier Guards of XXX Corps crosses the Veghel Bridge at 0715, it is observed by engineers of the 101st's 326th Airborne Engineer Battalion.

U.S. Army photo

XXX Corps advance ran into heavier opposition than expected, making its progress up the narrow road to Arnhem, soon named "Hell's Highway" by Allied soldiers, disappointingly slow.[1]

At 0615, September 19, 1944, the Bailey Bridge constructed at Son was completed and the first British tank of the Grenadier Guards Group of XXX Corps crossed. *U.S. Army photo*

Company C, 501st PIR, was ordered to send one platoon to Dinter. Reports from this company indicated the enemy was in some force in and around this town. The 3rd Battalion, 501st PIR, was ordered to move from Veghel to Eerde and take up a strong defensive position at that point. The remainder of the 501st PIR continued in a close-in defense of Veghel, and during the day the 2nd Battalion repulsed an enemy attack from the northwest estimated at more than 250 infantrymen. During the late evening, Company E was driven back from its outpost position about two hundred yards by a well-executed night attack by enemy parachutists.

The Dutch . . . were the finest folks I ever saw. I couldn't ask for any more cooperation than they gave us during the entire time we were in Holland.

—1st Lt. Sumpter Blackmon, A Company, 501st PIR

The 1st Battalion, 502nd PIR, continued in the defense of St. Oedenrode. The 2nd Battalion attacked at 0600 in another attempt to seize the highway bridge at Best. This attack was repulsed by the enemy. At 1415 the regiment, less the 1st Battalion, reinforced by

Paratroopers of the 101st Airborne Division watch as more tanks of XXX Corps pass by after crossing the Bailey Bridge. *U.S. Army photo*

one squadron of the 15/19 Hussars, launched a coordinated attack against the enemy position. This attack was very successful and the objective was seized at 1800. Fifteen 88mm guns were destroyed, 1,056 prisoners were taken, and more than three hundred enemy were left dead on the field after this battle. The 506th PIR established strong points east and west of Eindhoven and continued extensive patrols with the squadron of 15/19 Hussars attached. Private First Class Emmet Parmley of the 502nd recalled the excitement of the arrival of British tanks support:

> *When the English Churchill [tank] reached our line, it seemed everyone leaped out of their holes as if ejected by some force at the same time. We were all yelling and were*

Paratroopers from the 101st Airborne Division prepare to ambush a German patrol near St. Oedenrode. *Brothers in Arms: Hell's Highway screenshot*

In these reenactment photos, paratroopers from the 3rd Battalion, 502nd Parachute Infantry Regiment, set up a Browning M1919A4 .30-caliber light machine gun. The M1919A4 weighed about thirty-one pounds, was usually manned by a crew of two men (gunner and assistant gunner/loader), and had a rate of fire of four to six hundred rounds per minute. *Courtesy of Brian Perkins*

In this reenactment photo, a paratrooper is armed with a .45-caliber Thompson submachine gun. The Thompson was an excellent weapon for close-in fighting and one of the preferred weapons of the paratroopers.

Author photo

going to charge but the tank commander was a very calm person and said: "Let's not be hasty lads, perhaps we can give Jerry something to think about." At this time the tank was on our line at the left edge of the trees that led to the highway. He fired the big gun. It looked like an air burst just in front of the buildings on the highway. There were a few white flags but not many. He fired again. This brought results. The Germans on the left started surrendering as the tank moved across our front to the right of the trees that ran down to the highway and fired again on the right side of the trees. They started surrendering all up and down the line—so many that we just motioned them to the rear. They looked like good troops. Many had camouflage capes on, like the German paratroopers wore, but I did not see any paratrooper helmets on them.

One British tanker would give the 1st Battalion, 502nd, a new rally cry. The battalion, under the command of Lieutenant Colonel Cassidy, was held up on the road to Schijndel when they were joined by Sgt. James M. "Paddy" McCrory. McCrory's damaged tank, capable of going no faster than five miles an hour, had been forced to drop behind. Nevertheless, he joined in battle with 1st Battalion. He downplayed his contribution to the grateful paratroopers, saying, "When in doubt, lash out."

A third glider list began to arrive at about 1400 carrying the 1st and 3rd battalions of the 327th, the 81st Anti-Tank Battalion, the 377th PFA Battalion less Battery B, and the 907th and 321st Glider Field Artillery (GFA) battalions. Due to fog encountered en route, only a portion of these units arrived:

Weather and tactical developments produced several changes in the plans for D plus 2. . . . Weather conditions proved to be much worse than had been predicted. . . . The glider mission flown on D+2 by the 53rd Wing and 442nd Group for the 101st Division took off between about 1130 and 1320 in ten serials containing 385 plane-glider combinations . . . with visibility poor and clouds closing in at about 1,200 feet. . . . Glider pilots unable to see their tugs had to guide their craft by the tilt of the tow rope and by telephone conversation with the plane crew . . . 17 gliders had to be ditched in the Channel, but were located by rescue launches in time to save all personnel. . . . Of 213 gliders reaching the drop zone one was shot down, two or three crashed, and 209 made good landings. . . . Landings began at 1437 and ended about 1600. The mission had

Eduardo Peniche, 81st Airborne Antitank Antiaircraft Battalion: The 81st Arrives Late

Bad weather and the limited number of tow aircraft prevented us from departing, as planned, on D+1, Monday, September 18. We departed on Tuesday, September 19. Although the weather was still not favorable on D+2, we lifted off, in the fog, at 1300 hours on Tuesday, September 19. Our particular serial, carrying C Battery troops, was flying over a corner of London when I saw literally hundreds of other planes and gliders in the sky. It was then I realized that that was our RP (rendezvous point)—we were an "air armada"!—heading first toward the English Channel, then toward Belgium.

We were on double tow; our glider was carrying the AT (antitank) gun, and the piece was riding quite well. The other glider was carrying the prime mover, a quarter-ton Jeep. We also had six boxes of AT shells. I remember thinking about ack-ack (flak) fire. O'Toole sat in the copilot seat. Francis Papalio and Al Steen were across from me on the other side of the piece; I was riding on the so-called jump seat of the glider.

We reached our second RP, also called IP (initial point), somewhere near Brussels. From there we headed toward the target area, the landing zone (LZ) at Son. Through some clearings, we could see, on the highway below, long columns of British trucks and tanks heading toward Holland. I looked across and smiled at Frank Papalio; he smiled back and made a facial gesture, as if he were saying "We're going in!"

As we crossed into Holland, the ride started to get bumpy and "interesting." Before long we saw the "puffs" of ack-ack fire from German 88s, no doubt. Some of the explosions were quite visible. In the distance, to the left of our formation, a glider seemed to disintegrate in a big explosion; there were many small pieces falling from the sky. One of the tow planes was on fire, its glider cut loose. Joe O'Toole turned his head back and said something like "Hang on!" Suddenly, our pilot signaled that we were going to be released. There was a deep silence as we glided into the LZ. We were lucky—our landing was rough, but without serious damage. I saw a glider going into the trees; another one tilted to the left and crashed. Of the eighty-two CG-4A Waco gliders air-lifting the 81st Airborne Antitank Antiaircraft Battalion, only forty-seven reached the LZ that day.

We could hear automatic and rifle fire on the far side of the LZ. As we were getting the AT gun out, a couple of mortar rounds hit close enough that we could hear shrapnel cutting the air. It was about 1635 hours (4:35 p.m.); British and American fighters were strafing the enemy—this was combat in all its splendor! At about that time, two paratroopers from the 3rd Battalion, 502nd Parachute Infantry Regiment, reached us to offer assistance and information. It was right then that we learned that Lieutenant Colonel Cole, their battalion commander, had been killed in action the day before, near the DZ. They also told us that the main road was under enemy attack from both sides of the road. We had, in fact, landed uncomfortably near what was soon to turn into "Hell's Highway!" Now we were going to fight for it!

Eduardo Peniche, Fort Benjamin Harrison, Indiana, September 1943. Peniche was an AT gun crewman for a 57mm antitank cannon (designated a six-pounder by the British army). He was also the designated gunner to fire the bazooka for his squad. Concerning Operation Market Garden, Peniche reported, "We were very well trained for this mission and felt fully prepared for it. We were highly-motivated airborne soldiers who understood clearly the importance of our mission in going into Holland." *U.S. Army photo*

What It May Have Been Like: A Fictional Memoir of a Bazooka Man

Time: 1700 hours, September 19, 1944
Place: A road that heads east from the bridge at Son, Netherlands
Unit: 81st Antitank and Antiaircraft Battalion, 101st Airborne Division

I don't know where the Krauts suddenly got all the tanks. We were told that they were on the ropes, but they've scraped enough panzers together to make a big push all along this sector. In fact, this is the second night that Kraut tanks have pushed down this road into town, and we've blocked their advance and knocked out their vehicles. One of the tanks burning out on the road is one I hit.

I first heard of the M1A1 antitank rocket launcher—the bazooka—back in England, but I wasn't trained as a bazooka man. They thought that adding trained teams to the existing rifle companies would mess up all the army's logistical calculations. So they put five of these launchers on the company's books to be handed out as the situation required. I just happened to be nearest to the loaded bazooka when the panzers rumbled into our lines, so that made me our company's "bazooka man."

We have a lot of problems finding guys to use the bazooka because some say it won't knock out a bean can, let alone a German tank. I've never had a problem. The secret is to aim at a track, just above the running gear or at the back of the vehicle where the armor is thinnest, and you'll either immobilize it or scare off the tank crew. If the first shot doesn't penetrate, they won't want to hang around pushing their luck against me moving in and getting a better shot.

Tanks are usually supported by infantry, and they're my main worry. As a bazooka man, I'm officially supposed to carry just a pistol, but I've got myself an M1 carbine. It may not have the punch of the M1 rifle, but it's better than the pistol.

The bazooka is really simple in construction. It's just a length of tubing a couple inches in diameter with a shoulder stock and firing handle. The shoulder stock holds a battery that's connected to a cable that runs back to an insulated terminal at the

The fins of the bazooka rocket can be seen sticking out of the end of the tube in this photo. The rocket was 19.4 inches long and weighed 3.38 pounds. When the bazooka was fired, a stream of hot exhaust gas shot out from the back to a distance of twenty yards.
Courtesy of Brian Perkins

rear. The rocket is put into the launcher, the safety pin is pulled, and the stabilizer tube pushes all the way up to the notch in the fin. Between the fins is a single wire connected to the rocket motor at one end and to a small tab at the other. The tab is pulled through a spring onto the insulated terminal, completing the circuit once the trigger is pulled, igniting the rocket.

The biggest problem for the bazooka operator is the back blast from the rocket, which gives off a twenty-foot jet of flame as it travels down the barrel. It gives away the position of the launcher and can injure the loader if he gets in the way. This was a problem we found while fighting in buildings. The room was sealed when we shot, and it took us a week to pick the plaster and dirt out of our faces and hands!

Another problem with the rocket is that it's not always done burning by the time it leaves the barrel, so each launcher has a wire mesh cone to deflect the blast; they give us a small mask to protect the face and eyes. But the flash guards are too easily torn off in combat, and when you need to shoot the bazooka you don't have time to find a small mask—and a peppered face is the least of your problems!

The warheads are shape charged so that the blast is focused into a fine jet of gas and molten metal, which melts a hole in the armor plate, hopefully setting off any ammunition. Because all this occurs on impact, it doesn't matter about range just as long as you hit the target.

For a long while, a lot of bazookas were left behind, possibly because soldiers saw them

The bazooka was a close-range weapon. Although the maximum range of the bazooka was stated in U.S. Army field manuals as 400 yards, a good bazooka gunner was lucky to hit a target beyond 120 yards. *Courtesy of Brian Perkins*

as company weapons. Others said it was too bulky and impeded their movement. What most soldiers forget is that you can do more with a bazooka than just shoot vehicles. If you're held up by a sniper, you simply eliminate the room below him and that takes care of your problem! And I've heard that there is supposed to be a new bazooka that comes in two parts and screws together—

Wait. You hear that? Damn, the panzers are coming again!

Colonel Robert Sink (at left), commanding officer, 506th Parachute Infantry Regiment, issues orders to a paratrooper on the outskirts of Eindhoven. *Brothers in Arms: Hell's Highway screenshot*

carried 2,310 troops, of whom 1,341 reached their destination in safety, 11 were dead, 11 were injured, and 157 were missing. The remainder had been returned to England or landed safely somewhere short of the zone. Out of 136 jeeps loaded into the gliders, 79 arrived at the zone in good condition, as did 49 out of 77 trailers and 40 out of 68 guns.[2]

Elements of the 327th were given the mission of protecting the glider landing field and assisting the attack of the 502nd if necessary:

The 3rd Battalion attacking with the 502nd PIR toward Best (west) cleared the woods along the canal—the enemy retreated cutting across the battalion front. Seventy-five prisoners were taken, number killed and wounded unknown. One 88mm gun was knocked out. Our losses were three EM killed, three wounded and one missing. Company E of the 2nd Battalion was attached to the 3rd Battalion to defend the north and west portion of the landing zone.

The 1st Battalion left their departure fields in England at about 1130 and forty-three of the eighty gliders landed at approximately 1530. Heavy flak was encountered from the time the Albert Canal was crossed until the gliders landed. Several casualties occurred from flak and a few from rough landing. The 37 missing gliders landed either in Belgium, Holland, the English Channel, enemy territory, or returned to England. All but 8 of the glider loads were finally accounted for.

Of the C-47s in the flights, five were brought down in our sector by enemy aircraft fire.

After assembly the 1st Battalion was ordered to proceed to Son, Holland, where it was to defend the town and protect the crossing over the Wilhelmina Canal. The 2nd Battalion, less Company E, attacked enemy forces dug in about 3,700 yards west of Son at 1400 and encountered determined resistance on the canal. The attack was successful and 159 prisoners were taken. The battalion suffered only slight casualties.

—From 327th GIR, S-3 periodic reports for the period 18 September to 27 November, inclusive

At about 1700 enemy tanks and self-propelled guns were reported approaching Son from the southeast; the 502nd, while focusing on guarding its landing zone and on the fighting in Best, had left that approach lightly defended. A few minutes later, several tanks approached within a few hundred yards of the Son Bridge and shelled the bridge, the division CP, and the town. Technical Sergeant George Koskimaki noted:

Had a bad scare tonight when enemy tanks got within a couple hundred yards of the CP and shelled headquarters and the bridge over the canal. They apparently saw me run into the building with the message the enemy tanks were nearby. As soon as I got in the building, a shell crashed through the tile roof as I handed the message to an aide. They also fired on an observer who was in the tower beside the headquarters building. He came down in a hurry. Had General Ridgeway and General Brereton on my radio. General Ridgeway wanted to contact 18th Airborne Corps. I couldn't raise them with my SR-300 so I climbed on top of a chicken coop where contact was made immediately. Ridgeway climbed on the roof to talk to Brereton. I had to caution him about using clear text over the air.

By this time, however, the battle for Best had been won and the landings were finished, so the 502nd's forces were free to respond to the new threat. Little damage was done, and the German tanks withdrew when antitank guns of the 81st Battalion arrived from the glider landing field. Two tanks were knocked out by AT fire. Private First Class Ed Peniche of the 81st, who had been on the ground in Holland for only a few hours, remembered:

On that very first night in Holland, we were bombed near the bridge at Son. One thing I remember well is that Col. John Michaelis, the commander of the 502nd PIR, seemed to be all over the battle area. Shortly after he came to our AT (antitank gun) emplacement, we were ordered to fire a few rounds against the top of three windmills, which might have been used by the enemy as OPs (observation posts). Also, for good measure, we fired white phosphorous shells into some haystacks to set them on fire. There was a German half-track under one of them—another one had a tractor. As soon as we completed our fire mission, we moved to another emplacement.

At 1910 hours on September 19, 1944, the Luftwaffe bombed Eindhoven and caught a dense column of XXX Corps' trucks on the narrow roads of the town. In addition to several trucks destroyed, 227 Dutch civilians were killed and hundreds were wounded.

U.S. Army photo

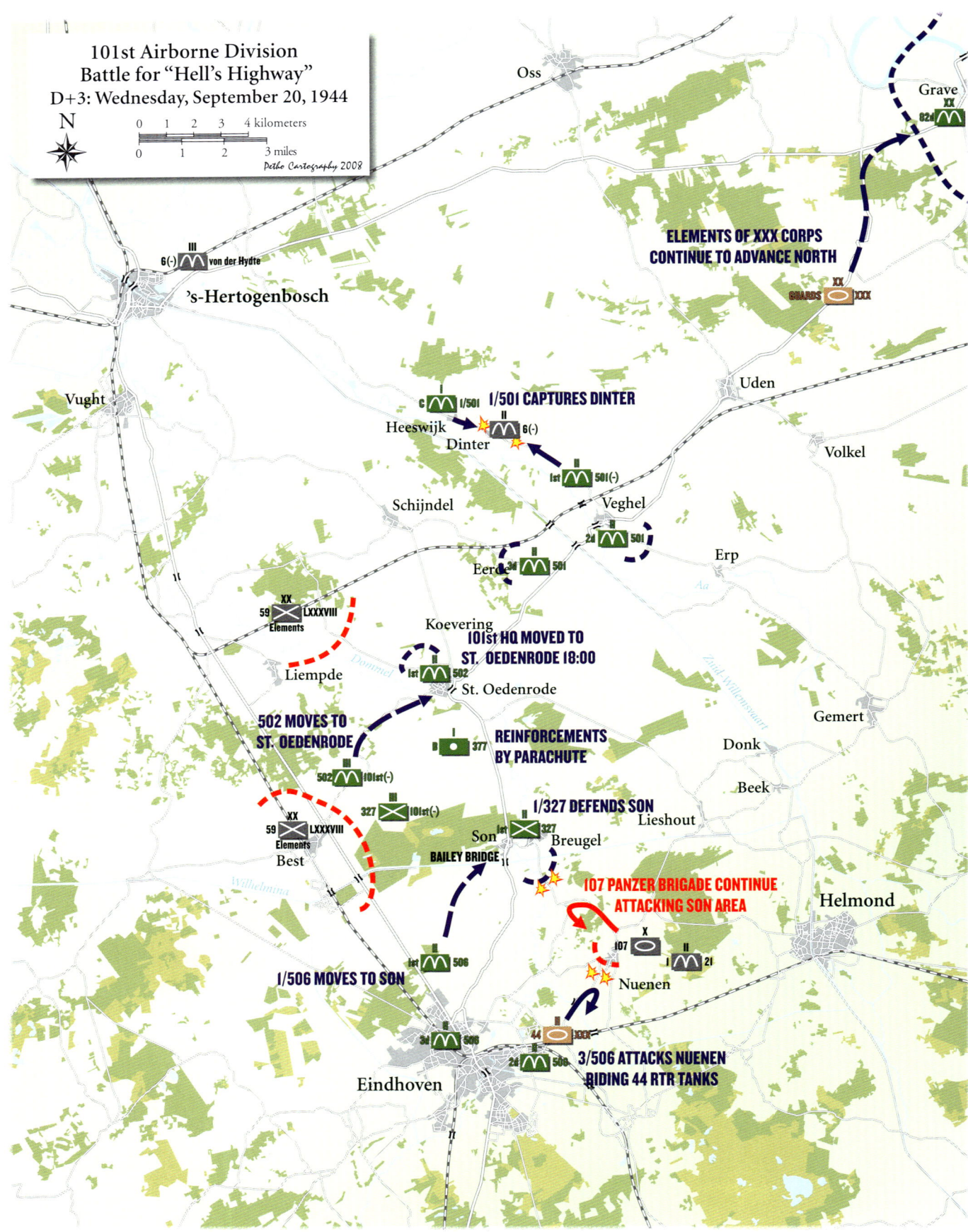

101st Airborne Division
Battle for "Hell's Highway"
D+3: Wednesday, September 20, 1944

N

0 1 2 3 4 kilometers
0 1 2 3 miles

Petho Cartography 2008

Oss

Grave
82d

ELEMENTS OF XXX CORPS
CONTINUE TO ADVANCE NORTH

GUARDS

's-Hertogenbosch

6(-) von der Hydte

Vught

Uden

1/501 CAPTURES DINTER

C 1/501
Heeswijk
Dinter 6(-)

1st 501(-)

Volkel

Schijndel

Veghel

2d 501

Erp

Eerde 3d 501

59 LXXXVIII
Elements

Koevering

101st HQ MOVED TO
ST. OEDENRODE 18:00

1st 502

St. Oedenrode

Gemert

Donk

Liempde

502 MOVES TO
ST. OEDENRODE

D 377

REINFORCEMENTS
BY PARACHUTE

Beek

502 101st(-)

327 101st(-)

1/327 DEFENDS SON

Lieshout

59 LXXXVIII
Elements

Best

Son 1st 327
Breugel

BAILEY BRIDGE

107 PANZER BRIGADE CONTINUE
ATTACKING SON AREA

Helmond

107
J 21

1st 506

Nuenen

1/506 MOVES TO SON

3d 506

44

24 506

3/506 ATTACKS NUENEN
RIDING 44 RTR TANKS

Eindhoven

82

CHAPTER 7

D+3: Wednesday, September 20

DURING THE NIGHT the 1st Battalion, 506th PIR, had been ordered to assist in the defense of the Son Bridge. By 0600 the 1st Battalion, 506th, along with elements of the 1st Battalion, 327th, and one company of the 326th Engineers, was in position. The German 107th Panzer Brigade attacked the bridge at about 0630. Riding tanks of the 15/19 Hussars, the 2nd Battalion, 506th PIR, attacked the enemy's rear lines in a skirmish at Nunen. The 3rd Battalion, 506th, stayed in Eindhoven as regimental reserve. The 44th Armored Regiment was attached to the division at 0900 and advanced toward Helmond in another move to defeat the enemy attacking the bridge. Sporadic tank and infantry fighting occurred throughout the day, but the attack was repelled.

The greatest stumbling block encountered by the Germans in combating Allied airborne operations in the West was the superiority of the Allied air force. German failure to eliminate this air force, or even to clear the skies temporarily, led to the most serious delays in bringing up reserves.

—From a German appraisal of Allied Airborne operations

A street scene in the town of Eindhoven, Netherlands, taken on September 20, 1944, shows the destruction of the German aerial bombing. *U.S. Army photo*

GERMAN TANKS IN ACTION

A German prisoner observes that the following are standard training principles in the German tank arm:

1. Surprise.

2. Prompt decisions and prompt execution of these decisions.

3. The fullest possible exploitation of the terrain for firing. However, fields of fire come before cover.

4. Do not fire while moving except when absolutely essential.

5. Face the attacker head-on; do not offer a broadside target.

6. When attacked by hostile tanks, concentrate solely on these.

7. If surprised without hope of favorable defense, scatter and reassemble in favorable terrain. Try to draw the attacker into a position that will give you the advantage.

8. If smoke is to be used, keep wind direction in mind. A good procedure is to leave a few tanks in position as decoys, and, when the hostile force is approaching them, to direct a smoke screen toward the hostile force and blind it.

9. If hostile tanks are sighted, German tanks should halt and prepare to engage them by surprise, holding fire as long as possible. The reaction of the hostile force must be estimated before the attack is launched.[1]

Two Screaming Eagles hit the dirt in a field in Holland in this reenactment photo. The near paratrooper, armed with a Thompson submachine gun, has an R painted on his helmet. The R on the side of this soldier's helmet designates him as a member of the Division Reconnaissance Platoon.

Author photo

Reports from the 327th summarized the action:

At about 0700 the Germans made an attack with infantry, accompanied by tanks, on the bridgehead south of the canal at Son. Three British and four German tanks were knocked out. German infantry crossed the river but were taken prisoner by our men or were killed. Eighty-five prisoners were accounted for in this battle. Units involved in this action were 1st Battalion, 327th GIR, and elements of the 506th PIR, 81[st Battalion], British troops, and tanks. At 1145 the 1st Battalion was ordered to clear the enemy from an area south of the canal between the Dommel River and the highway to a point 2500 yards south. The mission was complete by 1300 with more than one hundred prisoners taken.

The 101st Airborne Division command post moved from Son to the castle at St. Oedenrode at 1200. During the morning, the 1st Battalion, 501st PIR, under Lieutenant Colonel Kinnard, had attacked and seized Dinter, then moved toward Heeswijk, about four miles northwest of Veghel. The bulk of the battalion pushed infiltrating Germans back toward Heeswijk, where Kinnard had a

101st Airborne medics and a British soldier from XXX Corps hunker down with their wounded lying on stretchers in a ditch near Son as fighting rages up ahead on Hell's Highway on September 20, 1944. *U.S. Army photo*

company waiting. The classic encircling maneuver captured 418 Germans and killed 40, with the majority of the prisoners being air force personnel from improvised units. According to the historian Dr. John C. Warren, this "led the 501st momentarily to the rash conclusion that it had destroyed the enemy forces in its vicinity." The 2nd Battalion continued a close-in defense of Veghel. The 3rd Battalion conducted extensive patrolling to the north and west from a strong point at Eerde.

On the morning of D+3 (September 20, 1944), the Germans attacked again and we fought all day—until 1500 when our own tank attack with infantry stopped them. We had to scratch hard for infantry to go with the tanks.

—Lt. Col. Hank Hanna, assistant chief of staff G-3 (operations officer), 101st Airborne Division

Castle Henkenshage in St. Oedenrode served as the headquarters for the 101st Airborne Division from September 20–23, 1944. Tech Sergeant George Koskimaki is sitting behind the mound operating his radio.

U.S. Army photo

The 1st Battalion, 502nd PIR, continued the defense of St. Oedenrode. During the afternoon the 2nd and 3rd battalions were ordered to proceed to St. Oedenrode and the regiment charged with the defense of the St. Oedenrode area. By 2100 the entire regiment was closed in the area and had taken up strong defensive positions.

Our situation reminded me of the early American west, where small garrisons had to contend with sudden Indian attacks at any point along great stretches of vital railroad.

—Maj. Gen. Maxwell Taylor, commander, 101st Airborne Division

A British XXX Corps truck explodes after being hit by a German shell. Movement along Hell's Highway stopped after this, and trucks were stacked up on the road from Son to the Belgium border. *U.S. Army photo*

The 2nd and 3rd battalions, 327th GIR, relieved the 502nd of the defense of the sector east of Son and the landing zone and service area. The 321st GFA Battalion was attached to the 327th GIR and fired missions in support of that unit during the day. At 1500 Battery B, 377th GFA, arrived by parachute and joined its battalion. The 377th then moved to St. Oedenrode in support of the 502nd PIR. Battery A, 81st Antitank Battalion, was attached to the 327th GIR and Battery O to the 502nd PIR. Battery B remained in defense of the Son Bridge.

A Screaming Eagle sneaks up on the Germans near St. Oedenrode.

Brothers in Arms: Hell's Highway screenshot

U.S. Parachute Rifle Squad

The mission of the infantry is to close with the enemy by means of fire and maneuver to defeat or capture him, or to repel his assault by fire, close combat, and counterattack. During Operation Market Garden, success in battle hinged on the actions of platoons and squads in close combat—on their ability to react to contact, employ suppressive fires, maneuver to a vulnerable flank, and fight through to defeat, destroy, or capture the enemy. The rifle squad provided the basic building block of any infantry unit.

A U.S. Parachute Rifle Squad consisted of twelve men:

• Squad leader (sergeant/staff sergeant): The squad leader is responsible for everything the rifle squad does or fails to do. He is responsible for the discipline, appearance, training, control, and conduct of his squad. He leads it in combat, trains his squad to use and care for its weapons, to move and fight efficiently as individuals, and function effectively as a part of the military team.

• Assistant squad leader: The assistant squad leader performs duties assigned by the squad leader and takes command of the squad in his absence.

• Machine gunner: Carries and operates the M1919A4/A6 light machine gun or Browning automatic rifle (BAR).

• Assistant machine gunner: Carries the spare barrel and extra MG ammo.

• Eight riflemen: The core of the rifle squad, these eight men were usually armed with the excellent M1 Garand rifle.

Paratroopers move cautiously through a house as they search for German soldiers.

Brothers in Arms: Hell's Highway screenshot

Reports of the 327th GIR described the late afternoon:

At 1530 the battalion was relieved by the 506th PIR and moved across the canal and took up a defensive position along the west bank of the Dommel River, defending the area to their east.

The 2nd Battalion held its position of the preceding day. The 81mm mortar platoon captured four prisoners in the early morning. Company E rejoined the battalion from the 3rd Battalion, reporting one killed and three missing and five wounded.

The 3rd Battalion patrolled the Best–St. Oedenrode Road and protected the landing zone. At 1600 resupply by air was dropped by C-47s. During the day three prisoners were taken. The regimental supply section recovered most of the equipment and food dropped, although it was necessary to operate under enemy fire.

Differences between German and U.S. Infantry Tactics

In contrast to the doctrine of other nations, the German army holds that the machine gun, not the rifle, is the backbone of infantry tactics. The German squad is built around the light machine gun. It is the squad's base of fire. The riflemen support it and provide ammunition for it. In the U.S. squad, the riflemen are the base of fire, and the BAR (Browning automatic rifle) supports the riflemen. This may be one of the reasons why the Germans stayed with the K-98k rifle (designed originally in 1898 and modified last in the 1930s). In the U.S. squad the M1 rifle (adopted in the 1930s) was the newer weapon while their automatic weapon, the BAR (originally an 1918 design), was old. In the German squad, the MG34 (introduced in 1936) was the new design. The Germans even came out with a replacement for the MG34 in 1942 (the MG42).[2]

The German MG42 machine gun provided the German infantry an important firepower advantage in combat. In this reenactment photo, the machine-gun team consists of three men: gunner, assistant gunner, and ammunition bearer. *Author photo*

An American M1919A4 .30-caliber light machine-gun team fires at attacking German forces. *Brothers in Arms: Hell's Highway screenshot*

A German machine gunner fires on American defenders near St. Oedenrode. *Brothers in Arms: Hell's Highway screenshot*

Although that C-47 drop was successful, aerial resupply continued to have problems on D+3. Although thirty-five aircraft of the 442nd and 439th groups took off from Greenham Common and flew unharmed over the new southern route to DZ W at 1748, the drop was inaccurate. Only about 30 percent of their seventeen tons of supplies were recovered.

Still, at the close of the day, "Allied commanders believed success was still within their reach," according to Warren, at least as long as

the ground forces could strike north from the captured Nijmegen Bridge and reach the British airborne troops at Arnhem the next day. So far as they knew, the Arnhem Bridge was still in British hands. Defense of the salient against German counterattacks was obviously a prerequisite to a sustained advance toward Arnhem, but no serious threat to the salient was in sight.[3]

American paratroopers move supplies in a cart with the help of German prisoners as a British Sherman tank moves down Hell's Highway in Son.
U.S. Army photo

World War II U.S. Field Rations

- **C Rations** were composed of six key-opening cans (one day's ration), three meat or M-units, and three bread or B-units.
  - The M-units consisted of the M-1 unit of meat and beans; the M-2 unit of meat and vegetable hash; and the M-3 unit or meat and vegetable stew.
  - The B-Unit consisted of biscuits, a confection, sugar, and coffee, additional soluble beverages being added later.
- **D Rations** were vitamin-fortified chocolate bars containing chocolate sugar, oat flour, cocoa fat, skim milk, and artificial coloring; three four-ounce bars constituted a ration. This ration was only intended to be used for short durations, about one day, when no other ration was available.

- **K Rations** were a three-meal pocket ration consisting of the following:
  - Breakfast units: K-1 biscuits; K-2 biscuits; meat and egg M-unit; fruit bar; soluble coffee product; sugar cubes; cigarettes; chewing gum; and a can opener.
  - Dinner units: K-1 biscuits; K-2 biscuits; cheese product M-unit; confection; lemon juice powder; sugar cubes; cigarettes; chewing gum; matches; and a can opener.
  - Supper units: K-1 biscuits; K-2 biscuits; meat product M-unit; chocolate bar (field ration D); bullion powder; cigarettes; chewing gum; toilet tissue; and a can opener.

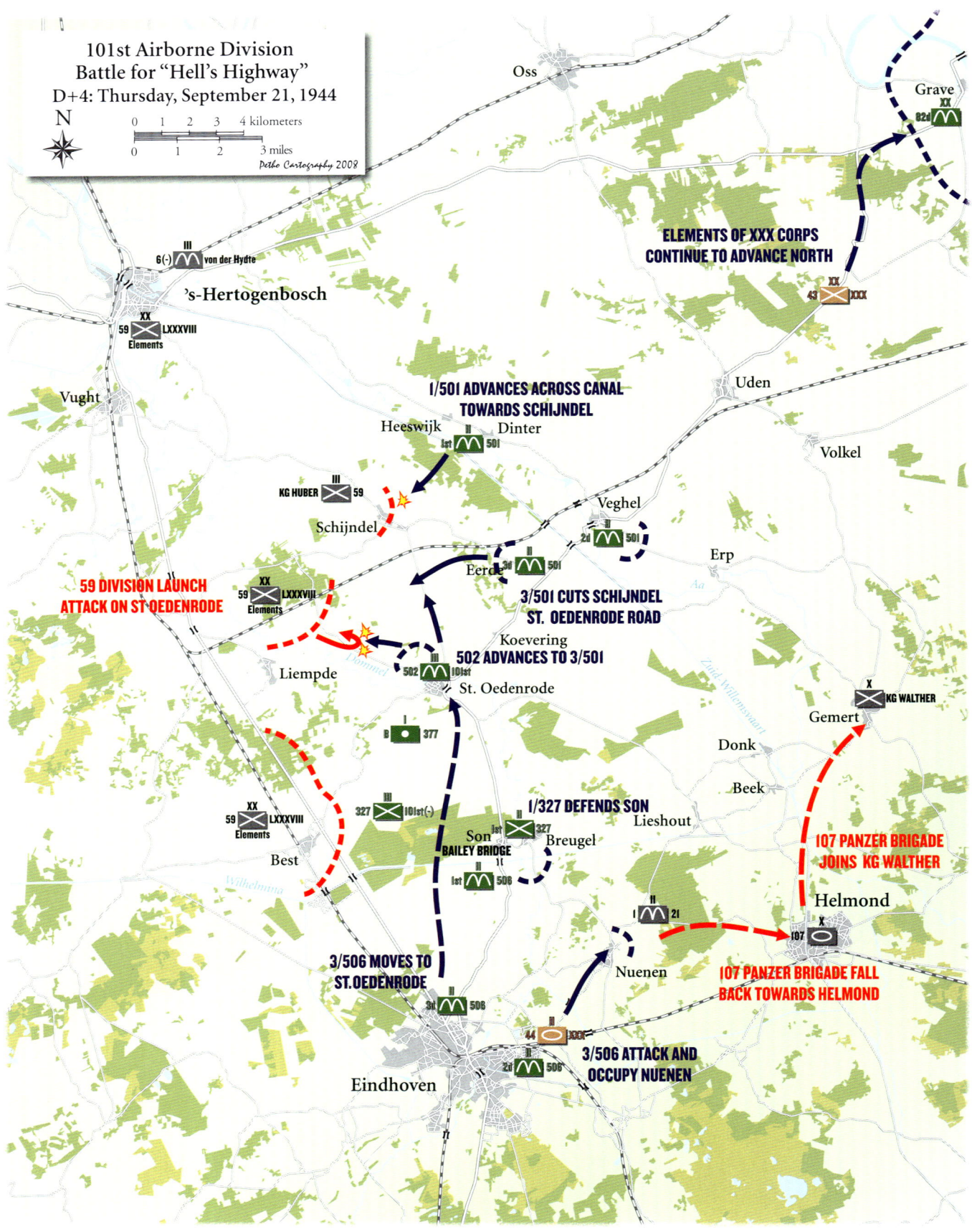

101st Airborne Division
Battle for "Hell's Highway"
D+4: Thursday, September 21, 1944

N

0   1   2   3   4 kilometers

0   1   2   3 miles

Petho Cartography 2008

Oss

Grave
82d

ELEMENTS OF XXX CORPS
CONTINUE TO ADVANCE NORTH

43   XXX

6(-) von der Hydte

's-Hertogenbosch

59 LXXXVIII
Elements

Vught

Uden

Volkel

1/501 ADVANCES ACROSS CANAL
TOWARDS SCHIJNDEL

Heeswijk   Dinter

1st 501

KG HUBER 59

Veghel

2d 501

Schijndel

Erp

Aa

Eerde

3d 501

3/501 CUTS SCHIJNDEL
ST. OEDENRODE ROAD

59 DIVISION LAUNCH
ATTACK ON ST OEDENRODE

59 LXXXVIII
Elements

Koevering

502 ADVANCES TO 3/501

502 101st

Liempde

Dommel

St. Oedenrode

Zuid Willensvaart

X KG WALTHER

Gemert

Donk

B 377

Beek

327 101st(-)

1/327 DEFENDS SON

Son 1st 327

Breugel

Lieshout

107 PANZER BRIGADE
JOINS KG WALTHER

59 LXXXVIII
Elements

Son
BAILEY BRIDGE

1st 506

Helmond

Best

Willehmina

II 2d

107

3/506 MOVES TO
ST. OEDENRODE

Nuenen

107 PANZER BRIGADE FALL
BACK TOWARDS HELMOND

3d 506

44 XXX

3/506 ATTACK AND
OCCUPY NUENEN

Eindhoven

2d 506

90

CHAPTER 8

D+4: Thursday, September 21

AT DAYBREAK, the 327th GIR gathered its remaining resupply. Patrols from all battalions took only light casualties and reported no further action with the enemy. Technical Sergeant Koskimaki of the 101st Airborne noted in his diary, "Moved division CP to St. Oedenrode last night. Aerial resupply dropped to us by low-flying C-47s. German fighters shot down two of them overhead. The crews didn't have a chance to bail out."

The 1st Battalion, 501st PIR, crossed the Zuid-Willemsvaart Canal in the early morning at Heeswijk and conducted extensive patrolling during the day. At 1845 an attack was aimed on Schijndel, and the northwest section of the town, with only minor resistance, was seized by approximately 2215.

So far fortune had favored us, but the sky was darkening. The Germans had been completely surprised by the initial airborne landings, but they had recovered quickly, and their countermeasures were now starting to take effect.

—Lt. Gen. Brian Horrocks, commander of XXX Corps, commenting on operations from September 17–21, 1944

Allied movement slowed to a standstill as the Germans cut Hell's Highway. Here, British soldiers guard a long line of Jeeps as the column waits for orders to move forward. *U.S. Army photo*

World War II Tactics 101

ENTERING BUILDINGS

One of our frontline leaders felt that it was better to enter the lower floors of buildings so that, if necessary, the building could be burned from the bottom; he was doubtless bearing in mind that the enemy could do the same if our troops were above. This platoon leader found also that after the ground floor was captured, a few AP shots (from an MI or BAR) upward through the floors would usually bring remaining enemy down with hands in the air. "When the enemy held out in a basement, a well-tamped charge of TNT on the floor above usually proved effective."[1]

Ubisoft/Gearbox Software

THE FOUR Fs

To win combat in World War II, squad leaders learned to distill tactics down to its basic elements. These basic elements are the four Fs: find, fix, flank, and finish the enemy.

Find the enemy first: Finding the enemy first gives a squad a tremendous tactical advantage, while blundering into an enemy is certain destruction. To find the enemy first, the squad leader must scout, or send a team, to check the ground before moving into potentially unsafe territory. A cardinal rule of squad tactics is to always engage the enemy on your terms, not his.

Fix the enemy with fire: Once the squad leader has found the enemy, he must quickly decide what to do next. In combat, a squad leader must use his understanding of the terrain, the team leaders' reports, and his knowledge of the enemy to make a tactical decision. The object is to deny the enemy freedom of maneuver by placing heavy and accurate fire on the enemy to pin him down.

Flank the enemy: Finding, forcing, and hitting the enemy's most vulnerable flank provides the squad with a battle-winning advantage. While a fire team suppresses the enemy, the squad leader leads an assault team to hit the enemy's flank. If the enemy appears to be too strong, the squad leader can withdraw the assault team and try another tactical approach. If the enemy seems weak, the squad leader might hold the assault team in position to suppress the enemy, fixing him with the team's fire, while he maneuvers his fire team to a position of advantage. Once you've hit the enemy's flank, he is "placed on the horns of a dilemma" because he is now receiving deadly fire from two separate directions. Finding a flank, or creating one, is the essence of World War II tactics and the central art to winning in combat.

Finish the enemy: The battle is not won until the enemy is finished off. As the fire team continues to suppress the enemy, the assault team maneuvers to destroy or capture the foe. Grenades, submachine guns, and carbines are the weapons of choice for the assault. As the assault team closes with the enemy, the fire team should shift fire to stop the enemy from moving away.

The 2nd Battalion remained at Veghel. The 3rd Battalion moved at 1745 to the west and cut the St. Oedenrode–Schijndel Road in the vicinity of the railroad station.

On 21 September ground operations went uniformly well south of Nijmegen and very badly north of it. By evening British units of VIII Corps advancing east of Eindhoven had taken the town of Geldrop and pushed on to the Wilhelmina Canal, thus belatedly freeing most of the 506th PIR for use elsewhere.[2]

A British Sherman tank from the 44th Royal Tank Regiment is knocked out by a German antitank gun near St. Oedenrode as it fights with elements of the 502nd Parachute Infantry Regiment to clear German forces from the road. *U.S. Army photo*

The 502nd PIR, with the 377th PFA Battalion attached, continued to expand its defensive positions in the St. Oedenrode area. Company B, 1st Battalion, received a strong enemy attack from the northwest in the early afternoon but held its position.

The 1st Battalion, 506th PIR, continued its defense of the Son Bridge. The 2nd Battalion, working with the 15/19 Hussars and the 44th Tank Regiment, attacked the enemy near Nederwetten. The enemy withdrew in the face of this attack, and at 1200 contact was lost. The 2nd Battalion went into a defensive position in the vicinity of Tonglere for the night. The 3rd Battalion was ordered to St. Oedenrode as division reserve. There was only limited enemy activity in the region of St. Oedenrode, a small and probing afternoon attack. The regiment was given a warning order that it would probably move to Uden on the following day.

Lieutenant General Horrocks pointed out that

British tanks of the 44th Royal Tank Regiment lined up front to back in the village of Veghel on September 21, 1944. The 44th Royal Tank Regiment supported the 101st Airborne Division in the battle to retain control of Hell's Highway. *U.S. Army photo*

the bulk of the German troops against us were hard-bitten Nazis from the SS and parachute divisions. Young fanatics had even advanced into battle sitting on the outside of their tanks shouting "I want to die for Hitler." The 101st U.S. Airborne Division guarding our life-line was being subjected daily to increasing pressure from both sides. Hardly a day passed without some fresh German formation making its appearance against us. No wonder, therefore, that on the next day, 21st September, the Guards Armored Division failed to advance more than two miles to the north. For once, air cooperation was working badly, and though the Typhoons were overhead, the contact-car could not get in touch with them. This was particularly unfortunate because very little artillery support was available.

COMBAT INFANTRYMAN BADGES

Description: A silver and enamel badge, one inch in height and three inches in width, consisting of an infantry musket on a light blue bar with a silver border, on and over an elliptical oak wreath. Stars are added at the top of the wreath to indicate subsequent awards; one star for the second award, two stars for the third award, and three stars for the fourth award.

Symbolism: The bar is blue, the color associated with the infantry branch. The musket is adapted from the infantry insignia of the branch and represents the first official U.S. shoulder arm, the 1795 model Springfield arsenal musket. It was adopted as the official infantry branch insignia in 1924. The oak symbolizes steadfastness, strength, and loyalty.

There are basically three requirements for award of the CIB. The soldier must be an infantryman satisfactorily performing infantry duties, must be assigned to an infantry unit during such time as the unit is engaged in active ground combat, and must actively participate in such ground combat.

An American moves north of Son to engage the Germans.

Brothers in Arms: Hell's Highway screenshot

Above: An American paratrooper from the 101st Airborne Division Reconnaissance Platoon readies his Thompson submachine gun as the sun sets north of the village of Son.

Brothers in Arms: Hell's Highway screenshot

The Sturmgeschütz, or StuG, was a series of German assault guns and tank destroyers produced by the Germans during World War II. Assault guns like the turretless StuG were cheaper to produce than tanks and could be manufactured in less time. As a result, the StuG was the most-produced German armored fighting vehicle, and German forces in Holland were armed with a number of StuGs like this Ausf G model StuG III. An excellent defensive weapon, the StuG had a high-velocity 75mm cannon that was very effective against Allied tanks. The StuG III was manned by a crew of four.

U.S. Army photo

Hawker Typhoon

At the time of the Typhoon's 1941 introduction, it was the RAF's first 400-mile-per-hour fighter. It could go head to head with the Focke-Wulf Fw190 but excelled in a low-level close-support role, attacking enemy airfields and communications across France, Holland, and Belgium beginning in August 1942. As the 2nd Tactical Air Force was built up starting in 1944, the number of Typhoon squadrons increased until by D-Day, when more than twenty-six squadrons were flying the plane.

Typhoon pilot Harry Hardy, Royal Canadian Air Force (RCAF), recalled his days in the plane during Operation Market Garden:

A strafing run started by lining up on your target at about a half-mile out, getting it squarely in your gunsight as you approached at about 400–500 mph, opening fire at 400 yards, fire about 15 rounds from each cannon, which was about a one-second burst, and pull up just missing the top of the target. The Typhoon would slow up as soon as you fired your cannons. You could feel it, because you'd go forward in your straps. It didn't take too many hits to knock out a vehicle or a train. If you hit, you hit with most of them. We'd report our results as flamers, smokers, or damaged. Flamers and smokers are obvious. Damaged means you saw your shells hit the target but it did not catch fire. When you see your tracers, then you've finished. The tracers come 20 rounds from the end. We kept those 20 rounds in case we got jumped by fighters on the way home.

Typhoons flew in standing patrols, or "cab ranks," during the European campaign, waiting for communications from ground forces to direct them to any German target in the way of Allied troops. They continued to disrupt enemy communications and transports (land and sea), proving to be an integral component in many of the later battles; they also achieved fame as tank destroyers. After the war in Europe was over, the need for the Typhoon's specialized role evaporated, and the plane was soon pulled from service.

The British Hawker Typhoon was one of the best ground attack fighters of World War II, especially when armed with four 60-pound RP-3 rockets under each wing. The Typhoon was especially effective during Operation Market Garden and was feared by German ground troops.

U.S. Army photo

Airmen of the British Royal Air Force load RP-3 76mm air-to-ground rockets with a sixty-pound tank-busting warhead on a Typhoon close-attack aircraft. The Typhoon, armed with these rockets, was a vital ingredient in XXX Corps' ability to blast its way up Hell's Highway.

Imperial War Museum

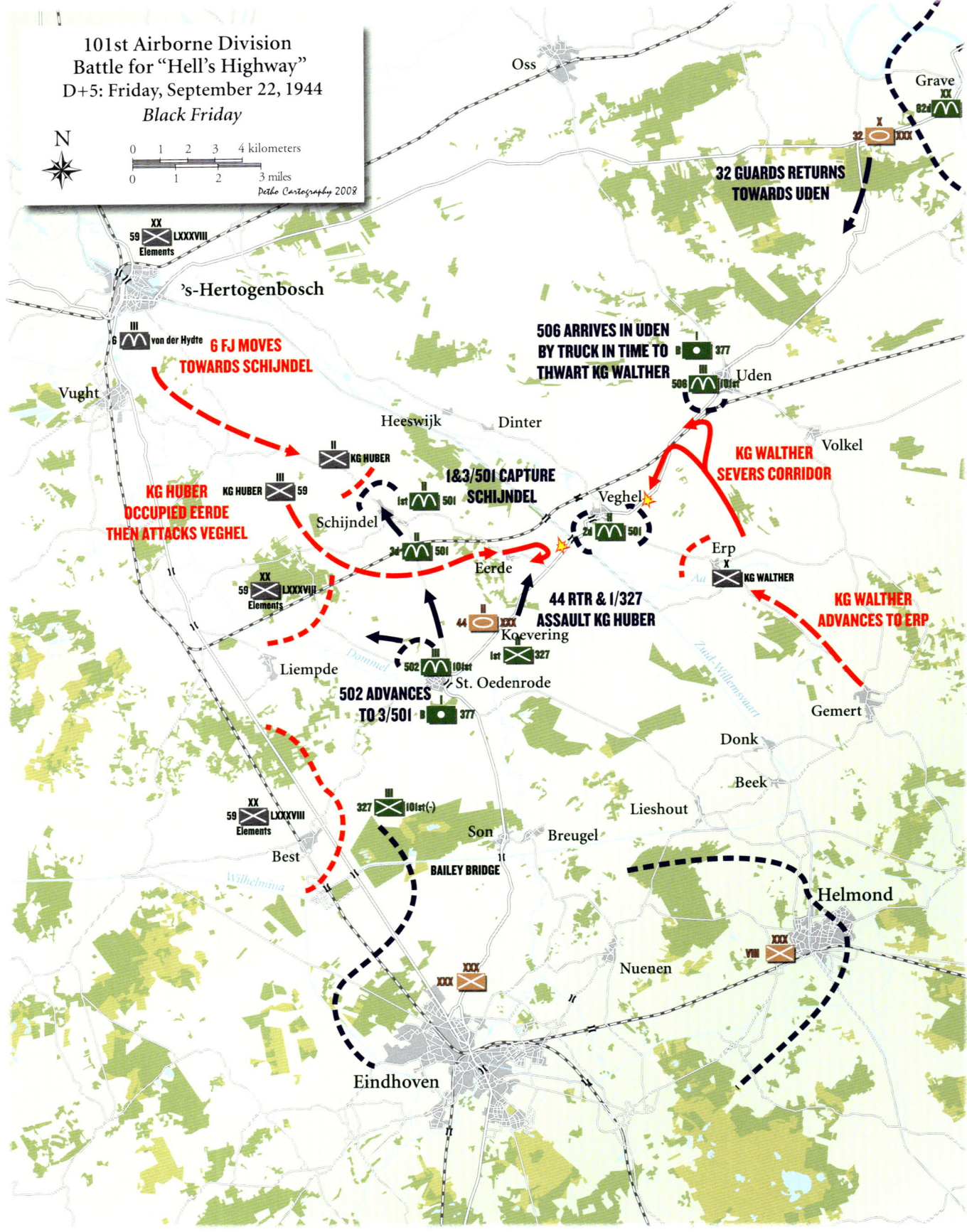

101st Airborne Division
Battle for "Hell's Highway"
D+5: Friday, September 22, 1944
Black Friday

N

0 1 2 3 4 kilometers
0 1 2 3 miles

Petho Cartography 2008

Oss

Grave
XX
82d

X
32

XXX

**32 GUARDS RETURNS
TOWARDS UDEN**

's-Hertogenbosch

XX
59   LXXXVIII
Elements

III
6   von der Hydte

**6 FJ MOVES
TOWARDS SCHIJNDEL**

Vught

Heeswijk   Dinter

**506 ARRIVES IN UDEN
BY TRUCK IN TIME TO
THWART KG WALTHER**

B
506   377

101st   Uden

Volkel

II
KG HUBER

III
KG HUBER   59

**1&3/501 CAPTURE
SCHIJNDEL**

1st   501

Veghel

**KG WALTHER
SEVERS CORRIDOR**

**KG HUBER
OCCUPIED EERDE
THEN ATTACKS VEGHEL**

Schijndel

II
3d   501

2d   501

Erp
X
KG WALTHER

XX
59   LXXXVIII
Elements

Eerde

II
44   XXX

**44 RTR & 1/327
ASSAULT KG HUBER**

Koevering

1st   327

**KG WALTHER
ADVANCES TO ERP**

Liempde

II
502   101st

St. Oedenrode

**502 ADVANCES
TO 3/501**

377

Gemert

Donk

Beek

Lieshout

III
327   101st(-)

XX
59   LXXXVIII
Elements

Best

Son

Breugel

BAILEY BRIDGE

Helmond

VIII

Nuenen

XXX

XXX

Eindhoven

CHAPTER 9

D+5: "Black Friday," September 22

AT 0300 THE 3RD BATTALION, 506th PIR, closed in on the St. Oedenrode area, moving up from Eindhoven. At 0500 orders were received that this battalion, as well as all other elements of the regiment, would move to Uden without delay. Movement was to be by motor and marching. The 3rd Battalion began its march to Uden at 0900. The 1st and 2nd battalions initiated their movements, piecemeal, as transportation became available during the day.

The advance detachment of the 506th PIR, consisting of approximately 150 officers and men from Regimental Headquarters and other units of the regiment, passed through Veghel at 1000 hours and continued on to Uden. Immediately after they passed through, the enemy cut the main highway between Veghel and Uden, and the detachment became isolated in Uden.

The Germans attacked the Corridor between Uden and Veghel from the east on 22 Sep and blocked all traffic for 24 hours. German forces launched several attacks on Veghel. All were stopped but the corridor is still cut. It is vital that Hell's Highway be cleared and to support the advance toward Nijmegen and Arnhem.

—Situation report September 23, 1944, from G-2 Section, 101st Airborne Division Headquarters

This reenactment photo shows some of the gear used by paratroopers during Operation Market Garden. The paratrooper standing and reading a map has a folding stock M1 carbine slung over his right shoulder. The M1 carbine fires a smaller and lighter .30-caliber (7.62mm) cartridge, different in design and performance from the larger .30-'06 used in the M1 Garand rifle. The M1 carbine was the most widely produced small arm in American military history with a total of 6.25 million models manufactured. *Author photo*

CRISIS AT VEGHEL, SEPTEMBER 22, 1944

On the night of the 21st and early on the 22d General Taylor, sensing the threat to his northern flank, gave orders for the 327th Glider Infantry Regiment to move to Veghel, and for the 506th PIR, minus the 1st Battalion, to occupy Uden four miles north of Veghel. About 1000 the regimental headquarters of the 506th rolled through Veghel, followed a little later by 175 men of the 2nd Battalion, and drove peacefully on to Uden. The rest of the 506th was still south of St. Oedenrode, and the 327th, which had not received its orders until 0930, was just starting. Only its 3d Battalion was to go by truck. The others were to march up back roads, so as not to block traffic on the highway. About 1100 the Nazis attacked Veghel in strength from the east, using the 107th Panzer Brigade and the 280th Assault Gun Brigade. This formidable force very nearly overwhelmed the single battalion opposing it, but the arrival at 1215 of part of the 2d Battalion of the 506th somewhat stabilized the situation. By frantic efforts the 3d Battalion of the 327th, the 3d Battalion of the 506th, and a battery of antitank guns were rushed in during the next couple of hours, and none too soon. At 1400 the Germans attacked again on the northeast, and at the same time the other arm of their pincer, several battalions of infantry supported by tanks and artillery, pressed from the west toward the canal bridges. Company D of the 506th, which had just ridden into town, was hastily dispatched to stop them and managed to do so with the support of a British tank squadron. Considerable British armor and artillery en route to Nijmegen had been held up in Veghel by the German offensive and played an important part that day in saving the town. Unable to break through into Veghel, the Germans used their superior numbers to work their way around the defenders and cut the highway both north and south of the town. Then they renewed their offensive, and very nearly reached one of the railroad bridges before being stopped. The pressure on the south was relieved about 1600 by the arrival of the main body of the 327th Glider Infantry and the 321st Glider Field Artillery Battalion. They fought their way into the town and took over the defense of its southwest side. Further insurance was provided by the return of the 3d Battalion of the 501st, which had been recalled from Schijndel at noon and marched into Eerde about 1630 after making a wide circle to the south. The crisis was over, but for several hours the enemy had been dangerously close to success, and the 101st Division had had to concentrate over half its strength to beat them off. Also the road was still blocked north of Veghel, and the detachment of the 506th in Uden was isolated under heavy pressure.[1]

The Germans attacked Hell's Highway between Uden and Veghel and blocked all traffic for twenty-four hours on September 22.

Brothers in Arms: Hell's Highway screenshot

LOOKING BACK, LT. GEN. BRIAN HORROCKS remembered the closed road as "the blackest moment" of his life; this was indeed Black Friday:

> *September 22nd was a worrying day for me. . . . The 1st Airborne had withdrawn west from Arnhem . . . While I was pondering this unhappy situation, the same staff officer arrived thirty minutes later with the news that a German armored formation had succeeded in cutting our road to the rear [Hell's Highway]. This was no fault of the 101st U.S. Airborne Division, who had been fighting a series of difficult battles to keep our lines of communications open. But it was no easy matter to defend some twenty-five miles of road with a resolute enemy pressing in on both sides. In fact, many stretches of the road were constantly under shell fire, and at times the banks on either side became the actual front lines facing outwards. As might be expected, this slowed up the traffic moving along the road considerably. . . . I was forced to turn the 32nd Guards Brigade back to start clearing the road from the north, while the 101st U.S. and 50th British Divisions advanced from the south. Though this operation eventually succeeded, for twenty-five fateful hours the road was closed to all traffic.*

This wasn't the only problem facing Horrocks on D+5. In addition to having to worry about the road behind them to the south, XXX Corps' progress northward to Arnhem ground to a halt. Horrocks explained what happened to Brigadier Essame, commander of the British 214th Infantry Brigade leading the drive toward Arnhem:

> *His orders had been to advance with all speed but, and this is important, he was told that artillery ammunition must be used with the utmost economy. Owing to enemy pressure on our lines of communication we were forced to economize as much as possible. . . . It was quite impossible for the 43rd Division to deploy armored vehicles in an attack across this difficult country intersected with high banks and dykes, in which the enemy enjoyed all the advantages of cover and the attacker none. So the Somersets advanced with practically no support at all either from tanks or guns.*

The German 107th Panzer Brigade, after withdrawing from its attack on the Son Bridge the previous day, had moved under cover of darkness to Erp and in the late morning of D+5, had launched an all-out attack to seize the town of Veghel and destroy the bridge there. Enemy forces in this attack were estimated as three battalions of SS troops supported by thirty to forty tanks and artillery.

An aerial view of Hell's Highway on September 22, 1944, showing the vehicles of XXX Corps backed up, bumper to bumper. *U.S. Army photo*

PARACHUTISTS' BADGES

Description: An oxidized silver badge 1 13/64 inches in height and 1 1/2 inches in width, consisting of an open parachute on and over a pair of stylized wings displayed and curving inward. A star and wreath are added above the parachute canopy to indicate the degree of qualification. A star above the canopy indicates a senior parachutist; a star surrounded by a laurel wreath indicates a master parachutist. Small stars are superimposed on the appropriate badge to indicate combat jumps as follows:

COMBAT PARACHUTIST BADGES

One jump: A bronze star centered on the shroud lines 3/16 inch below the canopy.

Two jumps: A bronze star on the base of each wing.

Three jumps: A bronze star on the base of each wing and one star centered on the shroud lines 3/16 inch below the canopy.

Four jumps: Two bronze stars on the base of each wing.

Five jumps: A gold star centered on the shroud lines 5/16 inch below the canopy.

Brigadier General McAuliffe, division artillery commander, 101st Airborne Division, meets with Col. Robert Sink, commander, 506th Parachute Infantry Regiment, to coordinate the defense of Veghel on September 22, 1944.

U.S. Army photo

[T]he weather was very bad and, after waiting until midday, Airborne Army cancelled all its missions. Fog had been widespread over England and the low countries throughout the morning and was replaced in the afternoon by stratus with ceilings about 1,000 feet and in places as low as 300 feet.[2]

By noon the 2nd Battalion, 501st PIR, astride the Veghel–Erp Road, was being hard pressed. Additional troops were started toward Veghel, and General McAuliffe was placed in command of troops in the area and charged with defense of the town and bridges. At about 1400, enemy tanks from the highway northeast of Veghel destroyed transport parked on the highway. Battery B, 81st Antitank and Antiaircraft Battalion, arrived at the same time, went into action on

This reenactment photo depicts a part of an airborne squad from the 1st Battalion, 502nd Parachute Infantry Regiment, halted at the side of a road.

Author photo

the highway, and immediately destroyed a Mark V tank leading the attack. Private First Class Ed Peniche of the 81st remembered:

> *On that day, D+5, September 22, 1944, the enemy cut the road between Veghel and Uden. The Germans attacked from both sides of the highway, from the east and from the west. Whoever baptized this road Hell's Highway had it right!*
>
> *As always happens during the firefight, the shelling and the automatic weapons fire was intensive. We were manning the gun and ready for the enemy armored and/or mechanized units. Frank Papalio and I were ready with our bazooka. We placed ourselves forward and ahead of the gun emplacement. During this attack our own 377th Parachute FA Battalion had its hands full supporting two regiments: the 502nd PIR and the 501st PIR, which had joined us in defending that sector of the highway. Additionally, we also had the mission of reopening the road and keeping it open!*

The 2nd Battalion, 506th PIR, took position on the left of the 2nd Battalion, 501st, with the 1st Battalion, 401st GIR, on its left. With the assistance of British artillery gathered from the highway, the attack from Erp was repulsed by dark. At about 1400, enemy infantry, with tank support, attacked astride the canal from the northwest toward the highway bridge southwest of Veghel. Company B, 506th PIR, which

The U.S. M2 60mm mortar provided flexible indirect fire support for American paratroopers fighting to keep Hell's Highway out of the hands of the Germans. The mortar weighed forty-two pounds, had an effective rate of fire of eighteen rounds per minute, and could fire a mortar bomb nearly one thousand yards. *U.S. Army photo*

IRON MIKE

Lieutenant Colonel John H. Michaelis, known as "Iron Mke," was a 1936 graduate of the U.S. Military Academy at West Point. He was an outstanding tactician and a highly respected leader who always led from the front. He assumed command of the 502nd PIR in June in Normandy, France, and led the regiment in Operation Market Garden. He was seriously wounded on September 22, 1944, "Black Friday," when a German shell exploded near him killing Pfc. Garland Mills and several staff officers. After healing from his wounds, he returned to the division during the Battle of the Bulge and was appointed chief of staff of the 101st Airborne Division in December 28, 1944. He served as chief of staff until the end of the war. After World War II, he served as aide-de-camp to Gen. Dwight D. Eisenhower and was publicly praised by Eisenhower as one of four lieutenant colonels in the army "of extraordinary ability." He commanded the 27th Infantry Regiment, the Wolfhounds, during the Korean War and was awarded the Distinguished Service Cross for heroism. He rose to the rank of general and served as the commander in chief, UN command/commander, U.S. Forces Korea/Commanding General, Eighth U.S. Army (CINCUNC/COMUSFK/CG EUSA) from 1969 to 1972.

was in Veghel on its way to Uden, was turned around, deployed near the bridge, and repulsed the attack, with the assistance of elements of the 44th Tank Regiment.

During the afternoon the enemy launched an attack against Veghel from the north and were finally halted just short of the railroad bridge by elements of the 2nd Battalion, 501st PIR, and one platoon of Company H, 506th PIR, which had taken up a defensive position there a short time before. Historian Warren explained the situation:

> *While British forces had moved up to buttress both flanks of the corridor as far as the Wilhelmina Canal, the road from [Son] to Grave was defended only by the 101st Division and by the British convoys moving along the highway. Over most of that stretch no man's land began at the edge of the road; off it in fields and farmyards and on obscure back roads, the enemy was concentrating his forces for a typical German pincer attack to snap the stem of the Allied salient. Veghel was the natural objective for such an attack, since destruction of the bridges there would block traffic for days no matter how soon the Allies retook the town. Furthermore, Veghel was lightly held. Its garrison, the 501st Parachute Regiment, had detached its 1st and 3rd battalions to carry on a little offensive of their own five miles away at Schijndel, leaving only headquarters and the 2nd Battalion to hold Veghel. The nearest source of reinforcements was the 502nd PIR at St. Oedenrode, and since it was needed to garrison that sector any substantial help would have to come from the Son area seven or eight miles away. The Germans could*

321st Glider Field Artillery Battalion on September 22, 1944

We were gradually pushing our way forward. On September 22, the battalion, given twenty minutes to "March Order," moved to a position southwest of Veghel to support the 501st Parachute Infantry. Elements of the Seventh Panzer Brigade plus the German infantry was hitting hard, aiming at cutting the supply route in that area. Shortly after getting these positions organized, the call came through to take up antitank positions at the bridge southwest of the town.

Skeleton crews went forward, and under direct observation and small-arms fire, remained there until ordered to displace to new positions along the St. Oedenrode–Veghel highway. Later reports were that enemy tanks had penetrated into the town, only to be knocked out by the Airborne 75s.

The battalion fired continuously in support of the infantry in repelling numerous counterattacks as the Krauts desperately tried everything they had in vain attempts to cut our supply route.

It was here that another very welcome sight appeared. Another Armada of C-47s pulling gliders. It was the 907th coming in. Too, the English were flying supplies and reinforcements to their surrounded and desperate comrades at Arnhem. Our fighter planes were giving these transports cover but the flak was intense. It was a sight that none will soon forget.[3]

fairly hope that by the time a relief column reached Veghel they would have the town.[4]

The enemy renewed their attacks from the south and southeast during the late afternoon, but by now additional forces had arrived and enemy attack was stopped. By dark the 506th PIR, less the detachment cut off at Uden; the 327th GFA Battalion; Battery B, 81st AT Battalion; the 2nd Battalion, 501st PIR; and the 1st Squadron, 44th Royal Tank Regiment, had arrived and formed the task force under General McAuliffe charged with holding the Veghel area.

101st has set up to resupply by air until D+3. Davis stayed back at Burg Leopold [Belgium] waiting for the trucks, but they arrived in driblets because of the traffic congestion and did not get forward until D+5.[5]

—Col. C. D. Renfro, 101st Airborne Division liaison officer to the British XXX Corps, September 1944

Barely visible beneath the wings of a Lockheed P-38 Lightning are the deadly bombs with which this multipurpose plane blasted German troops and tanks. P-38s like this one flew ground attack missions during Operation Market Garden. *U.S. Army photo*

The 1st Battalion, 501st PIR, had attacked Schijndel at dawn and had occupied all of the town by 0915. Some four hundred prisoners were taken in this operation. About noon, orders were received for the 1st Battalion to proceed to Weibosch, seize the town, and provide northern flank protection for Veghel. The movement was completed by 1700, and the battalion took up a strong defensive position in and around the town. The 3rd Battalion, which had advanced toward Schijndel in the morning and joined forces with the 1st Battalion in seizing Schijndel, was ordered to Eerde, where it took up a defensive position guarding Veghel from the west.

The 502nd PIR extended its defensive positions during the day. Elements of the 1st Battalion made contact with the 3rd Battalion, 501st, south of Schijndel, and joined forces in cleaning out several enemy strongpoints along the Schijndel–St. Oedenrode highway.

An American machine gunner prepares to fire on advancing Germans near **Veghel.** *Brothers in Arms: Hell's Highway screenshot*

This reenactment photo depicts two paratroopers from the 502nd Parachute Infantry Regiment in full combat gear. The paratrooper on the right carries an M1 Garand .30-caliber (30-'06) rifle with the M1 bayonet attached. A characteristic of the 502nd Parachute Infantry Regiment in Holland was the placement of a bandage on the front of the helmet, ready for quick use if a fellow paratrooper was wounded in battle. The entrenching tool of the paratrooper on the left is clearly visible. The entrenching tool was often as vital as a rifle—the paratroopers' ability to quickly dig in and tenaciously hold their ground became vital to keeping Hell's Highway open and repulsing German attacks. *Courtesy of Brian Perkins*

At 0930, the 327th GIR had been ordered to proceed to Veghel. The 1st and 3rd battalions were committed on both sides of the bridge immediately upon arrival; the 2nd Battalion continued into Veghel and became task force reserve. The town of Veghel was heavily shelled during the late afternoon and early evening. The 327th's periodic reports described the day's action:

The worst action I can remember was Veghel. . . . There was a dead GI lying at the main intersection of town, and when we came back in after being pushed out, some civilian had covered everything but his feet and legs with a raincoat and there was a small bunch of flowers which had been placed on his body. I was very touched by this act of concern.

—Pfc. James L. Martin, Company G, 506th PIR, remembering the fighting in Veghel on September 22, 1944

At 0930 the 1st Battalion was returned to regimental control. The regiment, intact with one battery of the 81 AB AA attached, was ordered to move to Veghel, Holland. Movement was started at 1030 by marching on foot. While en route the regimental commander received word of a German attack upon Veghel, which threatened the canal crossings. He at once ordered the antitank elements of the Regimental Headquarters Company and the battery of the 81st AB AA with two companies of the 3rd Battalion to move forward by motor vehicle ahead of the regiment. This group entered Veghel and defended the town on the north. The remainder of the regiment, marching on foot, found that the enemy ahead blocked the road just south of the Zuid-Willemsvaart Canal. The regimental commander ordered Company A of the 3rd Battalion and Company C of the 1st Battalion to attack on the west and east sides of the road while the remainder of the regiment continued the advance along the road. The attack was successful and the regiment crossed the canal, less the 1st Battalion, which occupied a defensive position to the south of the canal protecting either side of the highway leading into Veghel. Contact was made with the parachute elements within the city and a defensive plan agreed upon. During the attack of Companies A and C approximately 50 prisoners were captured.

Regimental Headquarters and Headquarters Company and the 2nd Battalion, [which were] initially regimental reserve, marched through Veghel to an assembly area in the fields northwest of the town. Shortly after entering the assembly area the enemy placed an intense artillery barrage upon the area, which lasted for approximately thirty-five minutes. It was apparent that the movement into the area had become known to the hostile artillery. Casualties were heavy—totaling eighteen dead and thirty-four wounded and evacuated. The reserve battalion and Regimental Headquarters and Headquarters Company was then moved to Leest, southeast of Veghel, occupying a defensive position.[6]

By dark on September 22, elements of the 101st Airborne Division and the 1st Squadron, 44th Royal Tank Regiment, took up positions to hold the area around the village of Veghel.

U.S. Army photo

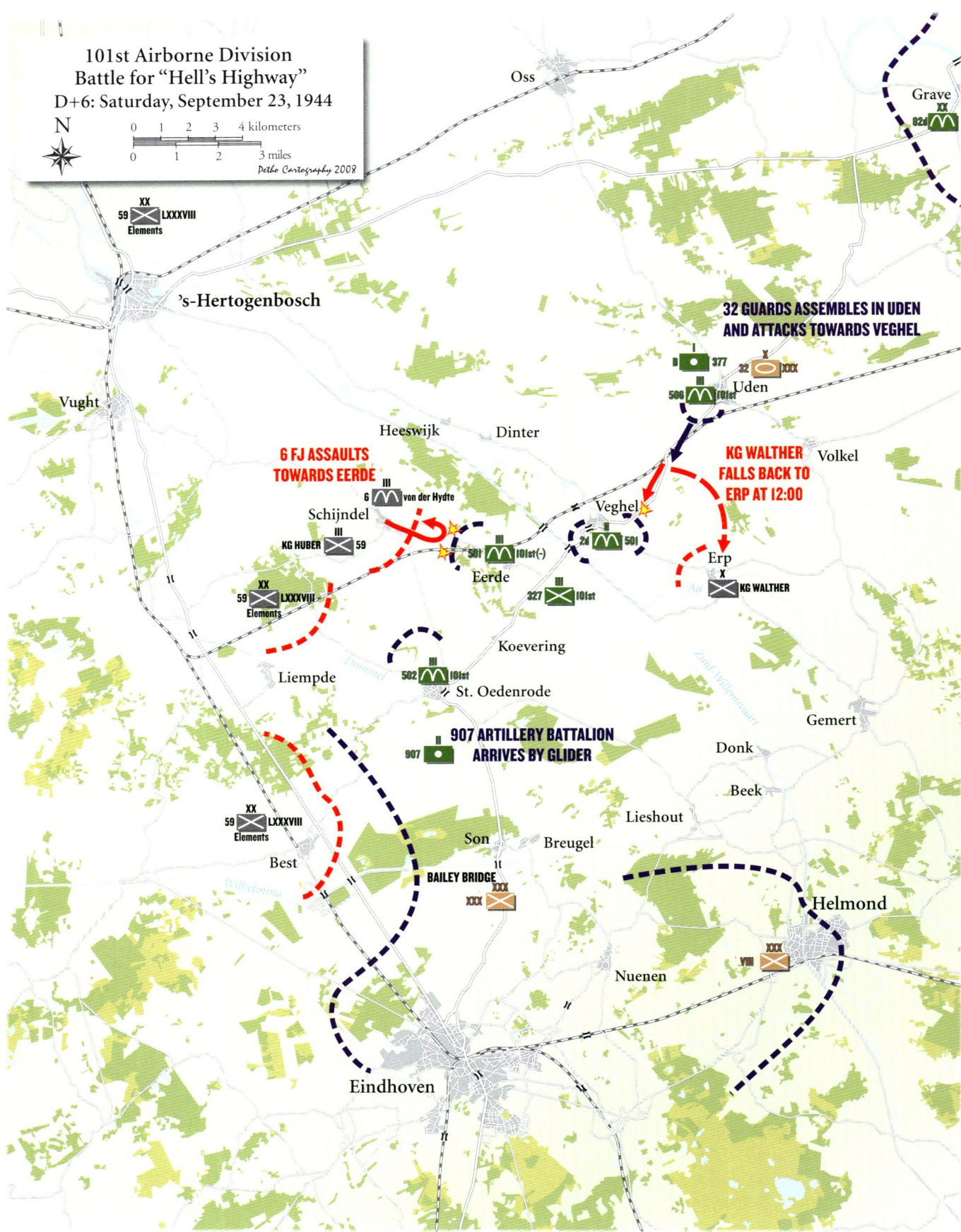

101st Airborne Division
Battle for "Hell's Highway"
D+6: Saturday, September 23, 1944

N

0   1   2   3   4 kilometers

0   1   2   3 miles

Petho Cartography 2008

Oss

Grave

82d

59 LXXXVIII Elements

's-Hertogenbosch

32 GUARDS ASSEMBLES IN UDEN AND ATTACKS TOWARDS VEGHEL

B 377

32

Vught

506 101st

Uden

Volkel

Heeswijk   Dinter

6 FJ ASSAULTS TOWARDS EERDE

6 von der Hydte

KG WALTHER FALLS BACK TO ERP AT 12:00

Schijndel

Veghel

KG HUBER 59

2d 501

501 101st(-)

Erp

Eerde

KG WALTHER

59 LXXXVIII Elements

327 101st

Aa

Koevering

Gemert

502 101st

Liempde

St. Oedenrode

Donk

907 ARTILLERY BATTALION ARRIVES BY GLIDER

907

Beek

Zuid Willemsvaart

Lieshout

59 LXXXVIII Elements

Son   Breugel

Helmond

Best

BAILEY BRIDGE

Wilhelmina

Nuenen

VIII

Eindhoven

106

CHAPTER 10

D+6: Saturday, September 23

THE GERMANS LAUNCHED SKIRMISHES against the defensive positions southeast of Veghel shortly after dawn. The small-scale attacks were easily repulsed. Plans had been made overnight to recall a British armored brigade from the Nijmegen area to advance on Veghel from Uden. The 32 Guards Brigade would meet up with the 2nd Battalion, 506th PIR, which would be approaching Uden from Veghel, and then they would clear the road for traffic. After completing that mission, the plan called for the 32 Guards Brigade to turn sharply south, cutting off the enemy from escaping through Erp.

Communication problems, however, kept the encircling movement of the brigade from happening as planned.

By 23 September, it was obvious to the Allies that Market Garden had run its course. German forces had stopped the advance of XXX Corps just short of Arnhem at Driel. The 1st British Airborne Division, cut off and suffering heavy casualties, received permission to withdraw.

—The Rhineland, CMH Pub 72–25, U.S. Army Campaigns of World War II

A squad of 101st Airborne paratroopers moves up the Veghel-to-Uden road. *U.S. Army photo*

ANTHONY CLEMENT McAULIFFE

Born in Washington, D.C., on July 2, 1898, McAuliffe was a student at West Virginia University (1916–1917) and graduated from West Point in November 1918. He advanced through the grades from second lieutenant in 1918 to general in 1955.

McAuliffe was commander of division artillery of the 101st Airborne Division when he parachuted into Normandy on D-Day and when he entered Holland by glider, in 1944. During Operation Market Garden he held the rank of brigadier general and played a critical role in the defense of Hell's Highway.

In December 1944, due to the absence of Gen. Maxwell D. Taylor, he was acting commander of the 101st Airborne Division and other attached troops during the siege of Bastogne, Belgium. When they became surrounded and the Germans demanded their surrender, he sent back a one-word reply: "NUTS." This is probably the most famous quote of World War II. In 1945, he commanded the 103rd Infantry Division until the end of the war in Europe.

Following the war, he held many positions including head of the Army Chemical Corps, G-1, and head of army personnel. He returned to Europe as commander of the 7th Army in 1953 and commander in chief of the U.S. Army in Europe in 1955. He retired from the army in 1956 and worked for American Cyanamid Corporation, 1956–1963. He served as chairman of the New York State Civil Defense Commission, 1960–1963. He resided in Chevy Chase, Maryland, until his death on August 11, 1975. He is buried in Arlington National Cemetery.

A wary paratrooper readies his Thompson submachine gun during the night fighting of September 23.

Brothers in Arms: Hell's Highway screenshot

NEVERTHELESS, THE 2ND BATTALION, 506th PIR, and the 101st counterattacked around 1500 hours, advancing northward from Veghel while meeting with little resistance. The 506th did make contact with a 32 Guards patrol northeast of Veghel about 1800, but by then the enemy had begun withdrawing and soon thereafter contact was lost. The brigade, after fighting its way down the highway from Grave to Uden, had found the advance detachment of the 506th PIR, which had been cut off in Uden the previous day, still holding its own. The highway was now open, and the trucks, held at a standstill for more than twenty-four hours, finally began to move.

Hell's Highway was strewn with wreckage from a British convoy, which the Germans had smashed the day before. The trucks were still burning.

—*Sergeant Schwenk, 101st Airborne Division*

101st Airborne paratroopers move past a burning truck in the town of Veghel. The Americans were desperate to reopen Hell's Highway as the British Airborne at Arnhem suffered terribly under German counterattacks. *U.S. Army photo*

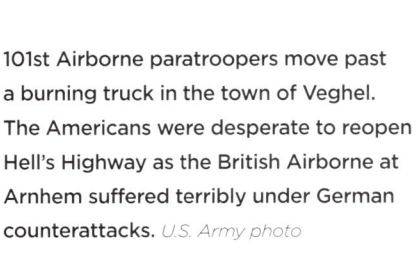

German forces, including this 88mm gun crew, launched several attacks on Veghel on September 23 (top and above). *Brothers in Arms: Hell's Highway screenshot*

German forces blocked Hell's Highway and destroyed several British trucks along the road.

Brothers in Arms: Hell's Highway screenshot

NEW GERMAN RIFLE FOR PARATROOPERS

The Germans have a new 7.92mm automatic rifle, the FG42 (Fallschirmjäger Gewehr 42), which is a light and versatile weapon, especially suitable for use by German airborne personnel. It should be remembered that t h e 9mm machine carbines (MP 38/40), which are now in general use, were originally introduced as parachutists' weapons; in like manner, the Germans may well put this new 7.92mm rifle to more general use in the future. The FG42 is air-cooled and gas-operated. In spite of the extensive use of stamping, instead of intricate machine-tool work, and in spite of the fact that all component weights have been reduced to a minimum, the new weapon is fairly sturdy. It is provided with a light folding bipod and a spike bayonet which, when attached, increases the overall length of the rifle from 3 feet 1 inch to 3 feet 8 1/4 inches. The feed is from a 20-round box magazine, which fits into the left side of the gun. The magazine may be loaded separately or from standard 5-round Mauser clips from the right side of the gun. The FG42 may well be used as a "powerful" machine carbine, as a "short range" self-loading rifle, or as a light machine gun when mounted on the bipod.[2]

The Fallschirmjägergewehr 42 (FG42) was a 7.92mm rifle designed for German paratroopers. The FG42 could fire in both semi-automatic and automatic modes. It had a twenty-round side-feeding magazine and was one of the most advanced rifles developed in World War II. Because of the complex nature of the FG42 design, manufacturing the weapon was difficult and expensive. Only seven thousand FG42s were produced by Germany in World War II. *Author photo*

IT'S A JEEP

I don't think we could continue the war without the Jeep. It does everything. It goes everywhere. It is faithful as a dog, as strong as a mule, and as agile as a goat. It carries twice what it was designed for, and keeps on going. It doesn't even ride so badly after you get used to it.

— *Ernie Pyle, World War II war correspondent*

A restored 101st Airborne Division U.S. Army World War II–era Jeep used by reenactors. *Author photo*

During the morning the 1st and 3rd battalions, 501st PIR, readjusted their defensive positions west and north of Eerde, and at dark they were deployed with the 3rd Battalion generally along the railroad from the Canal to Eerde and the 1st Battalion from Eerde due south to the main highway. The 2nd Battalion continued the close-in defense of Veghel, while the 506th PIR was given offensive missions to the northeast and south. The 327th GIR was busy: 1st Battalion, still in their position of D+5, engaged the Germans during the morning skirmishes, taking approximately twenty prisoners, while 2nd Battalion had a defensive sector south of Company F. At 1300 2nd Battalion relieved elements of 506th PIR west of Veghel, guarding the railroad bridge over the Zuid-Willemsvaart Canal. The 2nd, with Company E, advanced 1,200 yards over the bridge following an artillery barrage.

The 502nd PIR continued its defense of St. Oedenrode, with the 377th PFA Battalion in direct support.

The worst effect of the German roadblock was that it delayed the arrival of assault boats [badly needed by 1st Airborne]. . . . The renewed activity of the Allied air forces was a bright feature of D plus 6. Weather at last was favorable.[1]

During the day a fourth glider serial arrived, bringing remaining elements of the 327th GIR and the 907th GFA Battalion. These troops were moved immediately to the Veghel area, and the 907th was attached to the 506th PIR. The 321st GFA Battalion was attached to the 506th Infantry and fired several missions during the day.

Although the operation was not panning out as planned for XXX Corps, Horrocks still had this to say about his American allies:

As this difficult battle progressed, I became more and more impressed with the fighting qualities of the 82nd and 101st Airborne divisions. I learned afterward that they were the pick of the whole American army. What impressed me so much about them was their quickness to action; they were great individualists. They were also commanded by two outstanding men, the 101st by Gen. Maxwell Taylor, subsequently head of the U.S. Army, and the 82nd by Gen. Jim Gavin, until recently in charge of military research

The Projector Infantry Anti Tank (PIAT) was a British-designed and manufactured antitank weapon that used a spring to hurl a high-explosive antitank projectile at its target. This unusual weapon could not be reloaded easily, since it took a two-hundred-pound pull to cock the weapon. The PIAT's effective range was one hundred yards. *NARA photo*

A squad of American paratroopers patrols near a Dutch farm.

Brothers in Arms: Hell's Highway screenshot

While supporting paratroopers of the 101st Airborne Division between Veghel and Erp, this British Firefly of 44th Royal Tank Regiment was destroyed by German tanks from the 107th Panzer Brigade. The British crew got out without loss as the tank caught fire. *U.S. Army photo*

This Panther tank was destroyed by a British Firefly tank commanded by Lt. Wally Arsenault just before his tank was hit. The commander of the German 107th Tank Battalion, Maj. Hans-Albrecht von Pluskow, was killed in this tank. *U.S. Army photo*

321ST GLIDER FIELD ARTILLERY BATTALION, SEPTEMBER 23, 1944

In one mighty and costly effort the enemy did finally succeed in cutting the road, and our battalion with the 506th Parachute Infantry were completely cut off and surrounded for a period of two days. Our continuous firing together with the furious fighting of the 506th at last reopened the road. Keeping it so was a different story. This was done by using every available man. Artillerymen took over as machine gunners, bazooka teams, and riflemen. The battalion proved again that it could operate efficiently under the most trying conditions and still deliver prompt and accurate artillery fire whenever called upon.

Here we first became closely associated with the British army. They were forging through on the road that we had opened to their men at Arnhem. Bumper to bumper they came, seemingly not having a care in the world, taking time out to offer us tea and biscuits. They were truly a jovial lot. However, it wasn't long before they were to learn that driving at close interval was dangerous, especially in that country. Just north of Veghel they paid dearly for their mistake. Running into heavy resistance, one convoy was practically destroyed.

After the Veghel battle we moved north and went into position southwest of Uden. At 0300 hours the news was flashed that the enemy was counterattacking fiercely, trying again to cut the road. Crawling from our foxholes we made a forced march of eight miles back to Veghel. Arriving there just at daybreak, and just as we started putting our guns into firing position, the battalion was subjected to the most intense artillery and mortar barrage of the entire campaign. It was only through the fortunate finding of well-dug trenches and the able leadership of our battalion commander that the 321st was saved from annihilation. Pulling back a short distance, we soon had the guns firing and at once the attack was repulsed.[3]

and development in America. Both were as unlike the popular cartoon conception of the loud-voiced, boastful, cigar-chewing American as it would be possible to imagine. . . . Under their deceptively gentle exterior, both Maxwell Taylor and Gavin were very tough characters indeed. They had to be because the men they commanded were some of the toughest troops I have ever come across in my life.

In this reenactment, a paratrooper peers around the corner of a house in Veghel. The R on his helmet designates the 101st Airborne's Division Reconnaissance Platoon. The platoon was attached to division headquarters and normally conducted reconnaissance on enemy strength and movements for the division headquarters and S-2 section (Division Intelligence). In Holland, they were often attached to one of the PIRs for brief missions. *Author photo*

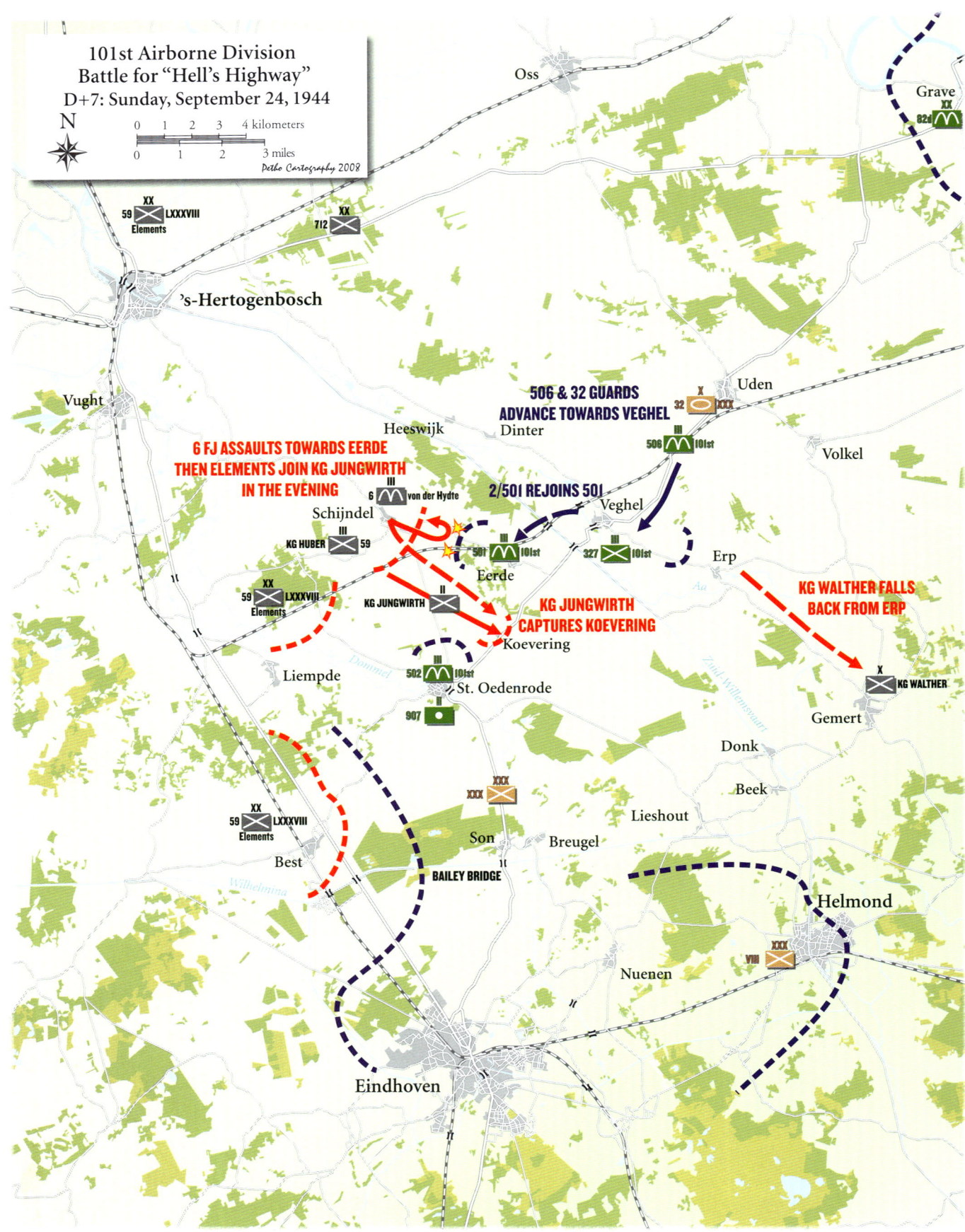

101st Airborne Division
Battle for "Hell's Highway"
D+7: Sunday, September 24, 1944

N

0 1 2 3 4 kilometers

0 1 2 3 miles

Petko Cartography 2008

Oss

Grave

59 Elements LXXXVIII

712

's-Hertogenbosch

Vught

506 & 32 GUARDS
ADVANCE TOWARDS VEGHEL

32

Uden

Volkel

506 101st

Dinter

Heeswijk

6 FJ ASSAULTS TOWARDS EERDE
THEN ELEMENTS JOIN KG JUNGWIRTH
IN THE EVENING

2/501 REJOINS 501

6 von der Hydte

Veghel

Schijndel

KG HUBER 59

501 101st

327 101st

Erp

Eerde

Au

KG WALTHER FALLS
BACK FROM ERP

59 Elements LXXXVIII

KG JUNGWIRTH

KG JUNGWIRTH
CAPTURES KOEVERING

Koevering

Zuid Willemsvaart

Liempde

Dommel

502 101st

St. Oedenrode

KG WALTHER

Gemert

907

Donk

Beek

Lieshout

Helmond

59 Elements LXXXVIII

Best

Son

Breugel

BAILEY BRIDGE

Nuenen

VIII

Wilhelmina

Eindhoven

CHAPTER 11

D+7: Sunday, September 24

AT DAWN reconnaissance as far as Erp indicated the Germans had withdrawn to the southeast, and the area was clear of enemy troops. The 506th PIR, with the 321st GFA Battalion and Battery B, 81st AT Battalion attached, was ordered to Uden to take over the defense of that area. The division command post was moved from St. Oedenrode to Veghel at 1000 hours.

About 0900 on the 24th the Nazis attacked at Eerde in a new attempt to cut the highway. The attack was repelled . . . and truck convoys were pouring up the highway. Encouraged by this turn of events, Dempsey [British 2nd Army commander] and Horrocks [British XXX Corps commander] . . . decided to make one more bid for victory.

— Airborne Operations in World War II, European Theater, *Dr. John C. Warren USAF Historical Division Research Studies Institute, Air University, September 1956, p. 145*

The bloody battle at Eerde, Netherlands, just southwest of the town of Veghel, was also a heroic victory for the 501st PIR. Paratroopers of A Company, 1st Battalion, 501st Parachute Infantry Regiment, repulsed a deadly German attack and captured these German machine guns.
U.S. Army photo

German prisoners of war captured during the fighting near Eerde on September 24, 1944. *U.S. Army photo*

THE 327TH GIR WAS ASSIGNED THE TASK of defending Veghel, with the 907th GFA Battalion in general support. According to 327th GIR reports:

> First and 3rd battalions ordered to move and during the preparation enemy action became strong at the withdrawal points and they were ordered back into former position. It was reported that the enemy had again cut the road at the city limits. Company G of the 2nd Battalion was attached to the 3rd Battalion.
>
> The 2nd Battalion was ordered to Erp, southeast of Veghel, to hold the bridge crossing until it could be blown by the British Engineers. During the move harassing artillery around the bridge and along the canal to the left. Company E set up two outposts, one on each side of the Bolst, tying in with Company G.

GERMAN GRENADES

The stick hand grenade, nicknamed the "potato masher" by American soldiers, was the standard hand grenade of the German army during World War II. The Stielhandgranate M24 (high-explosive stick grenade) was a modified World War I grenade with a pull cord in the hollow wooden handle, connected to a friction fuse (Brennzünder 24) and the detonator (Sprengkapsel 8). Before throwing the grenade, the soldier had to unscrew the metal cap at the handle's base to expose a bead fixed by a cord to the friction fuse. After grasping the bead and pulling the cord, the soldier had a delay of four and a half seconds before the TNT-filled head exploded.

The Stielhandgranate 43 was an M24-style grenade modified for easier production. The handle was solid and the pull delay fuse was located on top. It could be fitted with a fragmentation sleeve (Splitterring) to change the effect from concussion to fragmentation.

The Germans also used other types of "egg grenades," similar in appearance to Allied hand grenades.

From left to right: Stielhandgranate M24, with fuse pull in handle; Stielhandgranate 43, with blue-capped fuse at top and fragmentation sleeve; and concussion Stielhandgranate 43. *Courtesy of Gilbert Hoffman*

Three types of egg grenades, the later version having a ring for affixing to clothing or equipment. At right, the boxes for the friction fuses (metal box) and the detonators (cardboard box). *Courtesy of Gilbert Hoffman*

After the 2nd Battalion, 501st PIR, was released from its defensive assignment in Veghel it joined its regiment in the Eerde area, as regimental reserve. Battery A, 81st AT Battalion, continued attached to the 501st PIR, with the 907th GFA Battalion in direct support.

The 502nd PIR continued the defense of the St. Oedenrode area. Batteries D, E, and F, the antiaircraft batteries of the 81st AT Battalion, arrived in the seaborne echelon and were assigned to protect the division service area northwest of Son.

Back in England strong rains grounded troop carrier missions. Thirty-mile-an-hour winds lashed the airfields, and the overcast was unbroken from three hundred to eight hundred feet. Although the weather improved later in the day in the south of England, conditions still did not allow further troop carrier missions. The continuing difficulties with resupply and troop flights had kept Market Garden an uphill battle, especially considering the weaknesses of the Allies' opening position. Major General Taylor commented, "The initial ground mission of the division required its dispersion in three areas along a corridor about fifteen miles in length. This disposition made the Airborne troops weak at every critical point. . . . As it was, the issue hung in the balance on several occasions before the Airborne troops restored the situation."

At 1000 hours, the Germans launched a series of probing attacks against the defensive position, moving from Schijndel toward Koevering. Two companies of the 502nd PIR were dispatched to

The three most important man-portable antitank weapons of World War II. From top to bottom: the German Panzerfaust ("tank fist"); the German Panzerschreck ("tank terror"); and the American M1A1 Bazooka. All three were feared by tank crewmen. *U.S. Army photo*

The British Bren gun was a highly effective and reliable magazine-fed automatic weapon and was the primary source of infantry firepower in the British army in World War II.

U.S. Army photo

An American sniper views the enemy from a windmill near Koevering.

Brothers in Arms: Hell's Highway screenshot

THE U.S. WACO CG-4A GLIDERS USED BY U.S. TROOPS FOR MARKET GARDEN

A total of 13,909 Waco gliders were built in several locations in the continental United States, but primarily at the Ford Motor Company plant in Kingsford, Michigan. The Waco was a metal-framed glider that typically carried fifteen troops. The British-made Horsa glider was larger and could carry twenty-five troops. It could also carry small vehicles, antitank guns, or small howitzers. The Horsa was made primarily of wood, and approximately 3,644 were constructed during World War II.

Piloting a glider in combat was a harrowing experience. General William Westmoreland, who commanded artillery battalions in World War II and later went on to command U.S. forces in Vietnam, had this to say about the gilder pilots:

The intrepid pilots who flew the gliders were as unique as their motorless flying machines. Never before in history had any nation produced aviators whose duty it was deliberately to crash land, and then go on to fight as combat infantrymen. They were no ordinary fighters. . . . They were the only aviators during World War II who had no motors, no parachutes, and no second chances.

—*General William C. Westmoreland, U.S. Army, Retired*

This German self-propelled gun, a Sturmhaubitze 42, was knocked out by a paratrooper from the 377th Parachute Field Artillery Battalion near Koevering. The Sturmhaubitze 42, or StuH42, was an infantry support assault gun armed with a 105mm artillery cannon instead of the normal 75mm cannon found on the StuG III.

U.S. Army photo

How to Fight Panzers: A German View

An anti-Nazi prisoner of war, discussing the various methods of combating German tanks, makes some useful comments. Although they are neither new nor startling, they are well worth studying because they are observations made by a tank man who fought the UN forces in Italy.

German tanks undoubtedly are formidable weapons against a soft-shelled opposition, but become a less difficult proposition when confronted with resolution combined with a knowledge not only of their potentialities but also of their weaknesses.

When dealing with German heavy tanks, your most effective weapon is your ability to keep still and wait for them to come within effective range. The next most important thing is to camouflage your position with the best available resources so that the German tanks won't spot you from any angle.

If these two factors are constantly kept in mind, the battle is half won. Movement of any kind is a mistake that certainly will betray you, yet I saw many instances of this self-betrayal by the British in Italy. Allow the enemy tank to approach as close as possible before engaging it—this is one of the fundamental secrets of antitank success. In Italy I often felt that the British opened fire on tanks much too soon. Their aim was good, but the ranges were too great, and the rounds failed to penetrate. My own case is a good illustration: if the opposition had held its fire for only a few moments longer, I should not be alive to tell this tale.

By letting the German tank approach as close as possible, you gain a big advantage. When it is on the move, it is bound to betray its presence from afar, whereas you yourself can prepare to fire on it without giving your own position away. The tank will spot you only after you have fired your first round.

A tank in motion cannot fire effectively with its cannon; the gunner can place fire accurately only when the vehicle is stationary. Therefore, there is no need to be unduly nervous because an approaching tank swivels its turret this way and that. Every tank commander will do this in an attempt to upset his opponents' tank recognition. If the tank fires nothing but its machine guns, you can be pretty sure that you have not yet been spotted.

Consider the advantages of firing on a tank at close range:

1. In most cases the leading tank is a reconnaissance vehicle. Survivors of the crew, when such a short distance away from you, have little chance of escape. This is a big advantage, inasmuch as they cannot rejoin their outfit and describe the location of your position to the main body.

2. Another tank following its leader on a road cannot run you down. In order to bypass the leading tank, it has to slow down. Then, long before the gunner can place fire on you, you can destroy the tank and block the road effectively. Earlier in the war, a German tank man I knew destroyed eleven hostile tanks in one day by using this method.[1]

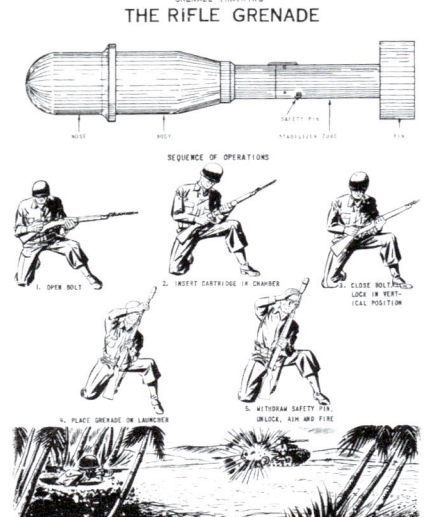

THE RiFLE GRENADE

SEQUENCE OF OPERATIONS

This diagram from a U.S. Army field manual explains the procedures for firing a rifle grenade. Rifle grenades gave the infantryman a close-in antitank and antipersonnel weapon with longer range than a hand-thrown grenade. Although rifle grenades were not effective against heavy German tanks, they could damage light armored vehicles. *U.S. Army photo*

Koevering to intercept this force, reported to be two tanks and about forty infantrymen. The German force moved rapidly and was almost in Koevering when Companies D and H of the 502nd PIR arrived. The two companies held Koevering but could not prevent the enemy from cutting the highway northeast of Koevering just before dark. Under cover of darkness, the enemy built up his forces with tanks, self-propelled artillery, and fairly large infantry units, using the corridor he had found between the 501st PIR and the 502nd PIR.

Must warn you unless physical contact is made with us early 25 September consider it unlikely [1st Airborne] can hold out long enough.

—*Major General Urquhart*

British Major General Urquhart, commander of the 1st British Airborne Division near Arnhem, sent a radio message warning that his forces would not be able to last beyond the morning of September 25 without reinforcements. When German tanks cut Hell's Highway once more that evening—blocking all movement north along the route—no chance remained that XXX Corps would reach the beleaguered 1st Airborne Division. The slow pace of XXX Corps' advance was a key element in the failure of Market Garden:

Undoubtedly, much of the trouble came because the British XXX Corps had to move some sixty-four miles to

American paratroopers take cover against a barn by a farmhouse near Veghel. "Kilroy Was Here" was a popular American expression in World War II and was expressed by GIs in graffiti around the world. *Brothers in Arms: Hell's Highway screenshot*

As shown in this reenactment photo, American paratroopers of the 101st Airborne carried a lot of combat gear, including rifles, ammunition, food, water, and a heavy pack. As they raced up and down Hell's Highway to stop the German assaults, the fatigue of nine days of intense combat began to tell. By September 24, 1944, both the Americans and the Germans were reaching the point of exhaustion.

U.S. Army photo

Arnhem over one main road, which was vulnerable to enemy attack. Instead of the expected two to four days, nearly a week was required for the advance to Arnhem. It is possible that the operation would not have been undertaken but for the Allied belief that the enemy between Eindhoven and Arnhem was weak and demoralized. One may readily believe that the Germans were right in concluding that the strength of the II SS Panzer Corps in the area was "a nasty surprise for the Allies."[2]

Nevertheless, on the evening of the 24th, the Allies had no choice but to continue the fight. Late that night, two companies of the British 43 Division and elements of the Polish Brigade crossed the Rhine in assault boats in a last-ditch effort to reinforce 1st Airborne.

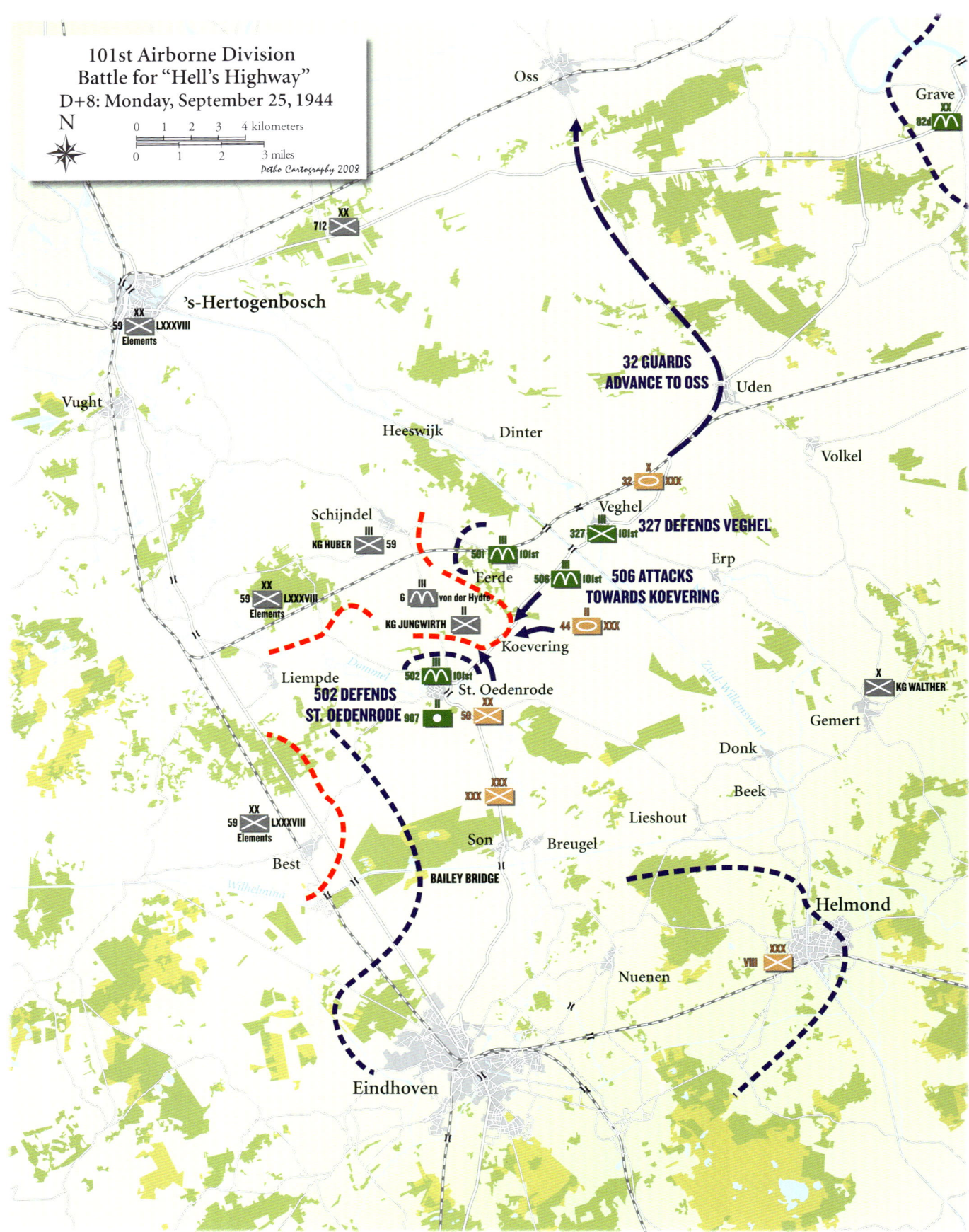

101st Airborne Division
Battle for "Hell's Highway"
D+8: Monday, September 25, 1944

N

0 1 2 3 4 kilometers
0 1 2 3 miles
Petko Cartography 2008

Oss

Grave
82d

712

's-Hertogenbosch
59 LXXXVIII
Elements

Vught

Heeswijk   Dinter

32 GUARDS
ADVANCE TO OSS   Uden   Volkel

Schijndel
KG HUBER   59

501 101st

6 von der Hydte
KG JUNGWIRTH

59 LXXXVIII
Elements

Veghel
327 101st   327 DEFENDS VEGHEL

506 101st   506 ATTACKS
TOWARDS KOEVERING

Erp

44

Eerde

Koevering

502 101st

Liempde

502 DEFENDS
ST. OEDENRODE
907

KG WALTHER

St. Oedenrode
50

Gemert

Donk

Beek

Lieshout

59 LXXXVIII
Elements

Best

Son   Breugel

BAILEY BRIDGE

Helmond

VIII

Nuenen

Eindhoven

CHAPTER 12

D+8: Monday, September 25

AS THE POLISH BRIGADE and 43 Division crossed the Rhine into the early hours of September 25, they had no hope of taking the strongly held Arnhem Bridge. They did, however, plan to make a foothold on the other side of the river and hold on until that night, awaiting further reinforcements. But the large crossing of reinforcements they expected would not come:

It was not for want of trying that we failed to arrive in time. . . . But after all we were cut off three times, and it is difficult to fight with one hand tied behind you. . . . The failure at Arnhem was primarily due to the astonishing recovery made by the German armed forces after their crippling defeat in Normandy.

—Lt. Gen. Brian Horrocks, commander of XXX Corps

British trucks from XXX Corps begin moving again on Hell's Highway on September 25, 1944. The German attacks at Eerde and Koevering on the 24th temporarily cut Hell's Highway and allowed German tanks to shoot up British truck columns like this one. *U.S. Army photo*

U.S. ARMY GRENADES

The U.S. Army used several different types of hand grenades in World War II. The most common hand grenade used by U.S. paratroopers battling along Hell's Highway was the MKIIA1, a fragmentation grenade commonly called the "pineapple" for its distinctive, serrated, cast-iron body. High-explosive (HE) versions used TNT instead of powder for explosive filler. While the fragmentation grenade was categorized as defensive for being especially effective when used from behind cover—protecting the thrower from his own shrapnel—the grenade had obvious offensive uses as well. The TNT-filled MKIII, with a laminated paper body, did not fragment and was classified as an offensive weapon.

MKIIIA1 offensive grenade with container and carrier pouch. The MKIIIA1 used TNT for its explosive.

Courtesy of Gilbert Hoffman

Grenade pouch, a practice MKII fragmentation grenade (blue) and an M15 white phosphorous smoke grenade with matching container.

Courtesy of Gilbert Hoffman

MKIIA1 fragmentation grenade (olive drab with yellow band), MKIIA1 high-explosive (HE) fragmentation grenade (yellow), MKIA1 training dummy grenade (black), low-explosive MKIIA1 fragmentation grenade (red), and matching container. HE ordnance was painted yellow until 1942, when the army switched to olive drab for camouflage purposes.

Courtesy of Gilbert Hoffman

Hardly had the plan been made when it was upset. At 0430 [September 25, 1944] the Germans slashed across the highway three miles south of Veghel. They brought up guns and tanks, and dug in for a long stay. It took forty hours to pry them off the road, and during that time Market strangled to death. The northward movement of all supplies and reinforcements was halted, but by far the most serious effect was the delay in the arrival of assault boats, without which even a medium-sized landing was impossible.[1]

In addition to the blocked highway, the missing assault boats, and bad weather continuing to restrict troop carrier operations, Panzers were reportedly moving up between the 1st Airborne and the Rhine, which would cut them off from reinforcements or escape. It was clear that 1st Airborne could endure no more. Montgomery gave the order for the airborne troops to withdraw south of the Rhine. Urquhart received the order by messenger at 0605, and preparations were begun:

On the morning of 25 September, the position of the 1st British Airborne Division had obviously become unten-able. Acting under the authority previously granted, the division prepared to withdraw that night. Beginning at 2200, the British brought more than 2,000 of the division and recent reinforcements south of the Neder Rijn. Some 6,400 of those who had gone in north of the river were dead or missing.[2]

Lieutenant General Horrocks, commander of XXX Corps, said:

When on the night of 25th September, the remnants of the 1st British Airborne Division were withdrawn south of the lower Rhine into our lines, all chance of finishing the war in 1944 was over. [Following Market Garden, the Allies captured a German analysis of the operation. The German report

This reenactment photo depicts a U.S. Army staff sergeant from the 1st Battalion, 502nd Parachute Infantry Regiment. He carries an M1A1 .45-caliber Thompson submachine gun with the standard twenty-round magazine. The M1A1 Thompson weighed 10.6 pounds and had an effective range of 75 meters. *Author photo*

A German Luftwaffe soldier lies dead by the side of the road along Hell's Highway near Koevering as an Allied truck passes by on September 25, 1944. Although the Screaming Eagles and the British armor repulsed the German attacks along Hell's Highway, the delay caused by these German attacks drew XXX Corps away from reaching Arnhem and decisively sealed the fate of the British and Polish Airborne. *U.S. Army photo*

stated the Allies'] chief mistake was not to have landed the entire First British Airborne Division at once rather than over a period of 3 days and that a second airborne division was not dropped in the area west of Arnhem.[3]

British lieutenant general Brian Horrocks, in a photograph taken in March 1945 at the crossing of the Rhine River. Horrocks was the brilliant and aggressive commander of the British XXX Corps, but in spite of his best efforts, he could not break through the German defenses to reach the British and Polish Airborne at Arnhem. In his autobiography, *A Full Life*, he stated: "Looking back I am certain that this was about the blackest moment of my life." *NARA photo*

During the previous night, the 506th PIR with Battery B, 81st AT Battalion, and the 321st GFA Battalion attached, had been ordered to return to Veghel from the Uden area. Movement began at 0300. on the 25th, and at daylight these units were just east of Veghel. At 0915, the 506th PIR, with one squadron of the 44th Royal Tank Regiment, attacked the Germans at Koevering. The attack progressed favorably for some two thousand yards, when both attacking battalions (formation, 1st and 3rd battalions abreast, astride the main road) were pinned down by well-directed artillery and small-arms fire, as well as fire from tanks dug in along the road. The 2nd Battalion was then ordered to execute a wide envelopment of the enemy's southern flank and began its movement at 1400. In the meantime elements of the 50th British

GERMAN RANK EQUIVALENTS

Wehrmacht (German army)	Waffen SS	U.S. Army
Grenadier	Schütze	Private
Obergrenadier	Oberschütze	Private First Class
Gefreiter	Sturmann	*
Obergefreiter	Rottenführer	Corporal
Unteroffizier	Unterscharführer	Sergeant
Unterfeldwebel	Scharführer	Staff Sergeant
Fähnrich	Standartenjunker	*
Feldwebel	Oberscharführer	Technical Sergeant
Oberfeldwebel	Hauptscharführer	Master Sergeant
Oberfähnrich	Standarten-Oberjunker	*
Stabsfeldwebel	Sturmscharführer	Sergeant Major
Leutnant	Untersturmführer	Second Lieutenant
Oberleutnant	Obersturmführer	First Lieutenant
Hauptmann	Hauptsturmführer	Captain
Major	Sturmbannführer	Major
Oberstleutnant	Obersturmbannführer	Lieutenant Colonel
Oberst	Standartenführer	Colonel
*	Oberführer	*
Generalmajor	Generalmajor	Brigadier General
Generalleutnant	Gruppenführer	Major General
General der ... (Infanterie, etc.)	Obergruppenführer	Lieutenant General
Generaloberst	Oberstgruppenführer	General
Generalfeldmarschall	Reichsführer	General of the Army

*no equivalent rank

Division, with strong armored forces, began an advance from the south.

By nightfall the Allies had drawn a noose about the Germans on three sides, but a small segment of Hell's Highway still was in German hands.[4]

The 501st and Companies D and H of the 502nd PIR assisted the attack by providing bases of fire for the attacking forces. By darkness the enemy had been cleared from all but a very small area south of the road, as related in the Operation Market Garden after action report of the 501st PIR:

During the night, the enemy, who had gotten into position on the exposed right flank of the regiment, had dug in on either side of the road and emplaced 88mm guns in concealed positions, with fields of fire down the highway. To open this, the only route of communication with the British army north of St. Oedenrode, one battalion, plus one company and ten tanks attached, attacked at dawn on the 25th. Almost immediately, four of the supporting tanks were knocked out by 88mm fire and the company accompanying the tanks was pinned down by small arms and fire from automatic weapons and artillery. Four more tanks were brought up to assist the advance, but were put out of action by enemy 88mm fire almost immediately upon getting into position. When the 88mm guns were spotted, friendly troops were so close to them that it was unsafe to bring artillery fire upon them. One 57mm AT (antitank) gun was brought up and laid on the 88mm gun, which was in a position behind a hedgerow near the road. Several hits were made on the 88mm gun, and it was put out of action. . . . In a firefight that lasted until 1800 hours the evening of the 25th, the enemy was pushed back bit by bit and finally forced to withdraw to the north thereby clearing the road in the battalion sector. The enemy suffered severe casualties in this action, and the many prisoners captured stated that it was their mission to cut the road and hold their positions at all costs.

The 502nd PIR continued its defense of the St. Oedenrode area, the 327th its defense of the Veghel area, and the 501st PIR its

A Screaming Eagle lies dead in the road as his comrades react to a German sniper in this reenactment photo. In a situation like this, one sniper could delay the movement along Hell's Highway for several hours. It was the job of the parachute rifle squad to find and silence snipers.
Courtesy of Brian Perkins

On September 25, 1944, near Koevering, this Sherman tank from the 44th Royal Tank Regiment was commanded by Lance Sergeant Walter Worley. His tank was supporting the 506th Parachute Infantry Regiment in an attack to push the Germans away from Hell's Highway when it was hit by a German Jagdpanther. Worley's tank caught fire, and he and two of the crew were killed. *U.S. Army photo*

German 88mm Dual-purpose Gun

The German 88mm dual-purpose gun (Flugabwehr-Kanone 8,8cm Flak 18, 36, and 37) was designed in 1934 and became one of the most versatile and deadly weapons of World War II. It served as antiaircraft flak gun (FlaK is a German contraction of the German word for antiaircraft gun), an antitank gun, artillery, and self-propelled artillery when mounted on a motorized chassis. The 88mm dual-purpose gun was highly effective in an antitank and antipersonnel role during Operation Market Garden. Using both HE and AP ammunition, the 88mm flak gun could destroy the heaviest Allied tanks at long range, up to two thousand meters. In antitank roles both HE (high-explosive) and AP (armor-piercing) ammunition was used with deadly effect against Allied medium and heavy tanks. The basic principle of German combat methods was adept fire and movement, with firepower increasing directly in proportion to the resistance encountered. German commanders learned to maximize the long range and lethality of the dual-purpose 88mm gun to a high degree, and this became a major factor in the employment of tank and antitank tactics in World War II.

A German 88 knocked out by Allied forces in World War II.
U.S. Army photo

defense of the Eerde area. All three regiments had several small-scale attacks launched against their positions during the day. Reports of the 327th summed up the actions of its battalions:

> *1st Battalion remained in positions defending the bridge at Veghel. Enemy artillery was heavy and many airbursts were seen.*
>
> *F Company of the 2nd Battalion established two outposts on the railroad northeast of the town of Veghel. E Company patrols were active during the night. F Company was ordered to the southeast of Veghel for defensive during the night.*
>
> *The Germans attacked the city of Veghel in force against the positions of the 3rd Battalion southwest of Veghel. At 0610, Company B reported that fifty persons approached within 150 yards when the men fired machine guns and mortars upon them, knocking out the entire unit. Enemy forces estimated at one rifle company attacked C Company but was driven off with heavy losses. At 1155, a force of three hundred enemy parachute troops supported by machine guns and howitzers attacked Company A's position and were held off. G Company of the 2nd Battalion was relieved and returned to 2nd Battalion control. The 3rd Battalion casualties for this date were four [enlisted men] killed, eighteen wounded, and two missing.*

Although the end of Market Garden was near, and both sides continued to scramble for the upper hand, Technical Sergeant Koskimaki was finally able to grab some time to make an entry in his diary:

I haven't had a chance to write in some time, but please bear with me. We are very busy at the present time. . . . Tank reinforcements arrived to help open the road this morning. The road is opened to armed convoys this afternoon. C-47s dropped a resupply of artillery ammo. The situation has cleared somewhat.

Much action took place between St. Oedenrode and Schijndel and Eerde on September 25th. The road had been cut northwest of Koevering on the evening of the 24th. The Germans were also pressing hard on the 501st positions in and around Eerde.

A German 88mm gun fires on a British tank as the 44th Royal Tank Regiment attacks the Germans near Koevering.

Brothers in Arms: Hell's Highway screenshot

During these late engagements, Sgt. Art Parker, 377th Field Artillery Battalion, 101st Airborne Division, became involved in action that earned him the Silver Star for his heroism. He was part of a bazooka team near St. Oedenrode and described what happened:

From our position, we could see only two [German] tanks but later found out there were six more behind them. The tanks could not get off the road due to the steep ditches on both sides. As the lead tank came into range, I let fly with the first rocket. It did not explode. This alerted the [German] infantry riding on the tank and they started firing our way. Lieutenant Shaw loaded another rocket into the bazooka and slapped me on the butt and I fired again. This time the rocket exploded right under the top track and the tank stopped. A lot of smoke but no fire or explosion inside the tank. The infantry bailed off the tank and ran up the road where our machine gunners opened fire on them as they took to the ditches. The second tank fired a few rounds in our direction and their machine guns sprayed the woods around us. We loaded the bazooka again and waited. The second tank moved up behind the dead tank and tried to nudge it off the road. All this time the cannon was moving from side to side in a menacing manner, looking for us while their machine gunner was cutting branches off the trees with his bursts. As the tank tried to push the other tank, it was almost stopped and Lieutenant Shaw gave me another pat on the butt and we put this rocket dead center in the second tank and it went up in smoke and flames.[5]

Paratroopers of the 101st Airborne Division approach a farmhouse as they patrol toward the village of Uden.

Brothers in Arms: Hell's Highway screenshot

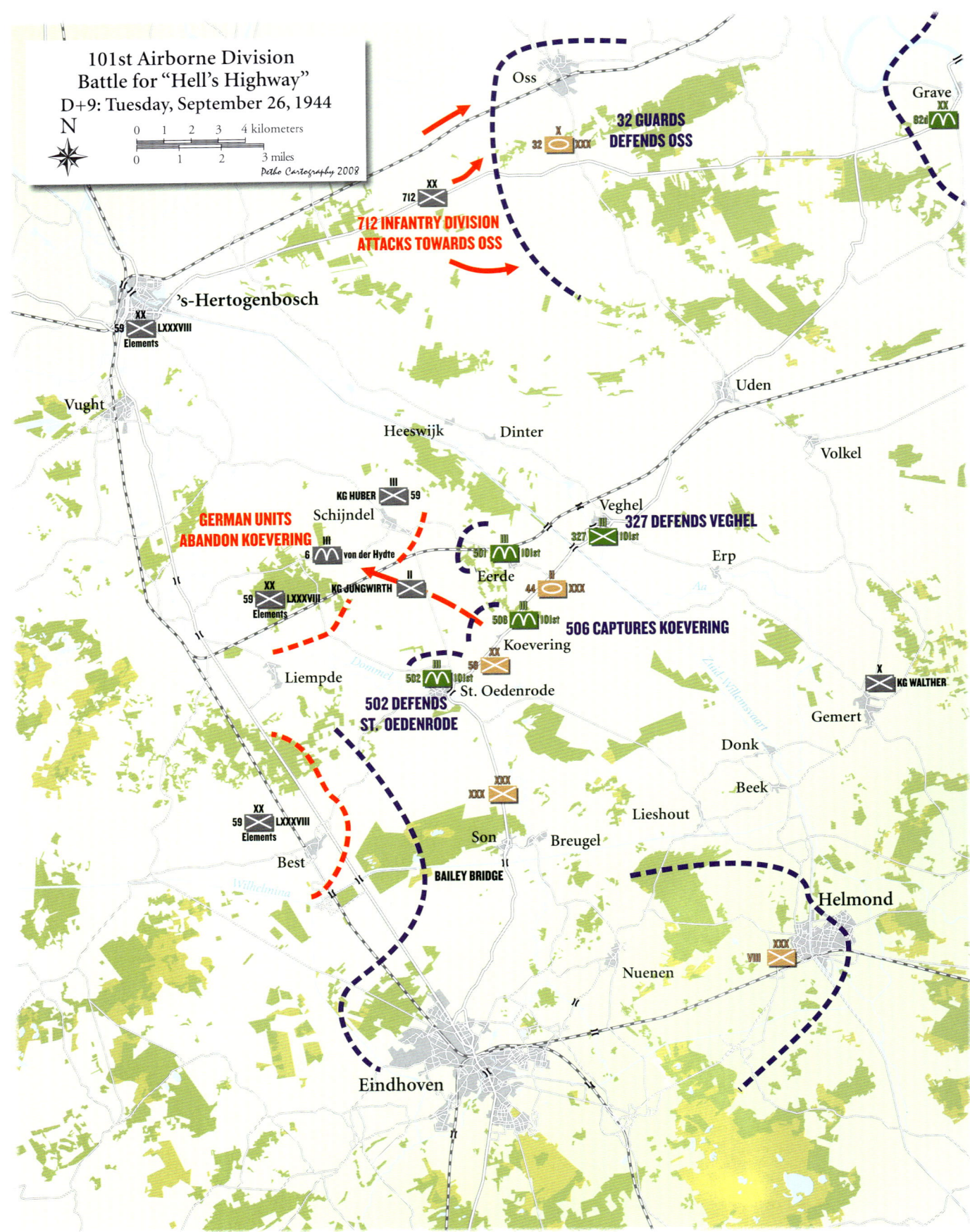

101st Airborne Division
Battle for "Hell's Highway"
D+9: Tuesday, September 26, 1944

N

0 1 2 3 4 kilometers

0 1 2 3 miles

Petho Cartography 2008

Oss

Grave

32 GUARDS
DEFENDS OSS

712 INFANTRY DIVISION
ATTACKS TOWARDS OSS

's-Hertogenbosch

Elements

Vught

Uden

Heeswijk   Dinter

Volkel

KG HUBER

Schijndel

Veghel   327 DEFENDS VEGHEL

GERMAN UNITS
ABANDON KOEVERING

von der Hydte

Erp

Eerde

Elements   KG JUNGWIRTH

506 CAPTURES KOEVERING

Koevering

KG WALTHER

Liempde

St. Oedenrode   Gemert

502 DEFENDS
ST. OEDENRODE   Donk

Beek

Lieshout

Elements   Son   Breugel

Best   BAILEY BRIDGE

Helmond

Nuenen

Eindhoven

130

CHAPTER 13

End of Mission

BY MONDAY SEPTEMBER 25, 1944, there was no doubt that Operation Market Garden had failed to achieve its objectives. Even the overly optimistic Field Marshal Montgomery, who called the operation a 90 percent success, realized that his dream to end the war before Christmas 1944 was not to be. By October, the 101st Airborne, assessing the operation in their official reports, stated that

the larger plan, of which Market was a part, failed because the Second British Army did not advance as rapidly as the plan envisaged. The reasons for its failure, and likewise the fortunes of the British parachute division which was to hold the northern sector of the corridor, and against whom the German counter-stroke fell most heavily, are to be sought in the records of the British army. Our men who saw them thought that their progress would have been more rapid and that the thing might have been done had they been less sparing of their infantry.

American forces . . . amply achieved [their objectives], though a glance at the map will show that the assignment . . . was beyond the compass of anything here-to-fore attempted by airborne soldiery. The 101st Division alone was given objectives strung out over about 22 miles of highway. . . [and] it was to capture . . . the large city of Eindhoven.

—*101st Airborne Division, September 1944, Operation Market Report, dated October 10, 1944*

This windmill bares witness to the ferocity of the combat that took place along Hell's Highway. *U.S. Army photo*

LIEUTENANT GENERAL BRIAN HORROCKS, commander of XXX Corps, did not shy away from the questions or accusations:

> *And so ended the battle of Arnhem. Now for the post-mortem. General Urquhart, the commander of the 1st Airborne Division, has complained that we were very slow in advancing to the relief of his division, and I can well understand his feeling. In fact his criticisms are perfectly reasonable when viewed from the airborne point of view. If I had been in his position, fighting desperately for eight days and always waiting for the 2nd Army which never arrived, I doubt whether I would have been half so reasonable. But if we were slow then the fault was mine because I was the commander.*

The post-mortem continues to this day, as historians and students of military history debate whether launching Market Garden was the correct decision. According to historian Charles B. MacDonald, "The operation was a daring strategic maneuver that failed. That the decision to launch it has not prompted the kind of controversy surrounding other command decisions is somewhat singular."[1]

Of course, just because the mission failed does not mean that it inherently had to fail. "Had the Germans not made one of the most remarkable military recoveries in history, it might well have succeeded," said Lieutenant General Horrocks. "How could we know then that 4th September was the fateful day when victory in 1944 slipped through our fingers?"[2] Certainly this is at the crux of the debate; one cannot really argue the controversy of launching the operation without weighing whether it was winnable. Field Marshal Bernard Law Montgomery said:

A 101st Airborne soldier guards two German prisoners of war in the closing days of September 1944. *U.S. Army photo*

> *In my prejudiced view, if the operation had been properly backed from its inception, and given the aircraft, ground forces, and administrative resources necessary for the job, it would have succeeded in spite of my mistakes, or the adverse weather, or the presence of the 2nd SS Panzer Corps in the Arnhem area. I remain Market Garden's unrepentant advocate. Seemingly, every Allied victory is an American success, every Allied defeat a British failure.*

Lieutenant General Horrocks sided with Montgomery:

> *Now let me turn to the 64,000 dollar question about which military historians will no doubt argue for many years. Was Monty correct in carrying out the Arnhem operation, which meant advancing sixty to seventy miles into Holland? Would it not have been better if, after Brussels, 21st Army Group had turned northwest and cleared both sides*

*of the Scheldt estuary to open the port of Antwerp, which
could then have been developed into a main base area,
thus curing many administrative headaches? . . . I can
only give you the opinion of a corps commander who was
on the spot and has since made a study of the problem. . . .
In my opinion Monty was right. . . . Arnhem was a
justifiable gamble.[3]*

Dutch Prince Bernhard, however, looked back on Market Garden
with a unique perspective, stating, "My country can never again afford
the luxury of another Montgomery success."

Let's review the facts. By late August 1944, the Germans were on
the verge of collapse in the west, and the Allies were optimistic that one
more hard push might bring the entire Nazi house of cards crashing
down. The Allies were advancing toward Germany on a broad front,
but there were not enough supplies to continue the attack with full
force everywhere. By September 1944, for serious logistical reasons,
the Americans and British were not prepared to exploit the German
collapse in the west along a broad front. The Allies had stretched
their men and machines to the limit and expanded their supply lines
from Normandy to the breaking point.

There was, however, the possibility of supporting one major attack
in one specific area. On September 4, Antwerp fell to the advancing
tanks of Montgomery's British forces, and spirits in the Allied camp
were buoyed with victory. Montgomery argued that one immediate
daring thrust, driven with relentless boldness and determination,
might cause the collapse of the entire German war machine. Seizing
the golden opportunity to thrust into what appeared to be a huge,
vulnerable gap in Holland, General Eisenhower decided to launch his
strategic reserve and reinforce Field Marshall Montgomery's recent
battlefield success. On September 10, Market Garden was approved.

Time is the critical factor in war, however and once lost
cannot be regained. The planning, preparation, and execu-

Paratroopers of the 101st Airborne Division check for German antitank mines on a road on "the island" in October 1944. German casualties from Operation Market Garden were 3,300 casualties (killed, wounded, and captured as admitted by German field marshal Walter Model) although other estimates put the figure as high as 8,000. *U.S. Army photo*

In the fall of 1944, the Screaming Eagles had to contend with mud and cold as well as the Germans on "the island." *U.S. Army photo*

tion of a major attack like Market Garden takes time. During the vital first week of September 1944, the western Allies paused as Montgomery's plan evolved. Even though the plans and preparations were conducted at breakneck speed—all in seven days—this time lost was time gained by the Germans. In this short period, the Germans created a miracle and reorganized and repositioned their meager forces. In the very nick of time, the Germans moved forces into Holland and plugged the gap.

Although there were several important intelligence indicators that the chaos of August was over, no one on the Allied side was completely aware that the Germans had regained their balance. Market Garden, therefore, was launched on September 17, 1944, and almost everyone on the Allied side believed it would be a huge success.

Huge is a good description of the combined airborne and ground attack into Holland. The scale of the Market Garden effort was truly gigantic. The parachute echelon of the 101st Airborne Division alone consisted of 436 C-47 transport planes carrying some 6,809 paratroopers of the division. There were 424 planes dropped on D-Day, and 12 planes carrying Battery B, 377th PFA Battalion, with 140 personnel and six guns, dropped on D+3. A total of 988 CG-4A Waco gliders took off from departure bases over a period of seven days. A total of 667 of these gliders landed without incident on the designated LZ.

The 101st Airborne Division had the critical job of securing the base from penetration. The division's missions called for the seizure of the four highway and railway bridges over the Aa River and Zuid-Willemsvaart Canal at Veghel; the seizure of the highway bridge over the Dommel River at St. Oedenrode; the seizure of the highway bridge over the Wilhelmina Canal at Son; and the seizure of Eindhoven and the main highway bridges over the streams in that city, all spread over a road distance of some twenty-two miles.

The planes carrying the 101st encountered heavy antiaircraft fire as they approached their targets, but the pilots were able to hold formation, and the paratroopers, for the most part, were delivered to the correct drop zones. Once on the ground, the Screaming Eagles secured their objectives and took the town of Eindhoven and linked up with the British XXX Armored Corps the following day, September 18. So far, so good, and the locals were certainly willing to help:

FINDING LIEUTENANT SHAUVIN
Linda Shauvin, Daughter of Lt. Eugene Shauvin

First Lieutenant Eugene P. Shauvin was the sixth C-47 aircraft in a six-plane flight of Pathfinders of the 501st Parachute Infantry Regiment of the 101st Airborne Division. His mission was to drop these Pathfinders on Drop Zone A, near Veghel, Netherlands. His C-47 tail number was 981.

When letters to my mother stopped in late September, she became distraught, fearing the worst. Then one of her letters to him was returned, the enveloped marked "missing in action." On October 27, 1944, she received an official telegram notification from Adjutant General J. A. Ulio notifying her that he was "missing in action." One year later she received notification that my father's status was changed to "missing in action and presumed dead." This was her final notification.

It wasn't until 1999 that I started the detective work that eventually brought closure on what happened to my father. After posting a note on a C-47 website, I was contacted by World War II researcher, David Berry of Dayton, Ohio, who put me in touch with Col. Charles Faith, jumpmaster on my father's aircraft. Colonel Faith was stunned to receive a phone call from the daughter of the pilot of the aircraft he had last seen going down in flames with some of his men aboard fifty-seven years ago. He was very emotional and said: "Gene's daughter! He was a wonderful man and a fine pilot." He told me the entire story of how their C-47 was hit by German flak, was burning, and how my father and his copilot did their best to allow the Pathfinders to exit the aircraft before they crashed.

Colonel Faith put me in touch with the nephew of one of the paratroopers whose contact from the "Dutch Friends of U.S. Airborne" had located the crash site. The next year, with Dave Berry's masterful research file in hand, I presented our case to the U.S. Army's Central I.D. Lab (CILHI) at Hickam Airforce Base, Hawaii. Out of seventy-eight thousand still missing from World War II, they chose our case, and in September 2003, excavated the crash site. They found and

Second Lieutenant Eugene P. Shauvin (left), standing with his navigator, 2nd Lt. John "Jack" Richards, taken by Gene Wilger at Chalgrove Airbase, England, on the morning of September 17, 1944, before they took off on Operation Market Garden, never to return. *Linda Shauvin*

identified debris from the plane, but did not recover any human remains.

On September 17, 2001, fifty-seven years to the day of my father's death, my mother was finally presented with a U.S. flag. The entire town of Retie, Belgium, turned out for the dedication of the memorial commemorating the sacrifice of the men of aircraft 981.

During my odyssey, I learned that my father, like so many of his generation, had a vast reservoir of courage and commitment to the cause of his country and winning the war. When my mom asked him why, as a married man, he felt he should volunteer for such hazardous duty, he said, "Because I have you and Linda and that gives me so much more to fight for."[4]

101st Airborne soldiers bury their dead after the battle for Hell's Highway in the temporary cemetery at Wolfswinkel between the villages of Son and St. Oedenrode. *U.S. Army photo*

The temporary cemetery at Wolfswinkel eventually contained 416 graves. The 101st Airborne Division suffered 2,110 casualties during Operation Market Garden with 752 killed in action. *U.S. Army photo*

Unforgettable! There we were standing eye to eye with our liberators . . . . Sympathetic men, out of another part of the world, come all the way to us, risking their own lives! And everything that happened in the moments after that was as in a dream. We had to talk with our hands and feet. Unfortunately, the language was a big problem. Especially the leaders of the paratroopers were anxious to get information from us about "where to . . ." They lost their awareness of direction. Most of them had a map and compass but they were on strange territory full of enemies.

—Liza Van Overveld, who lived in Son and was fourteen years old in 1944, remembers her first sight of American paratroopers from the 101st Airborne Division

On September 17, the 82nd Airborne Division had landed to the north to seize the bridges in and around Nijmegen, Netherlands. The 82nd, after hard fighting, also secured its objectives. The British 1st Airborne and the Poles jumped near Arnhem to secure the bridge across the Rhine, the bridge "too far."

The British XXX Corps had attacked on September 17 from the Belgium border toward Eindhoven and, after an initially tough fight, linked up with the 101st on the 18th and the 82nd on the 19th. XXX Corps then continued the attack up the single road to reach the British 1st Airborne at Arnhem. It was now a race against time and control of the bridges along eighty miles of a narrow strip of highway to Arnhem.

The Germans, however, quickly recovered from their initial shock. They surrounded the British Airborne in Arnhem and quickly counterattacked the American 101st and 82nd Airborne divisions. As the British tanks fought north, the Germans focused their counterattacks to block the narrow route and stop supplies from getting forward to the lead British units. During the days that followed, the 101st and 82nd Airborne fought desperate battles against determined German counterattacks to control the road and stop the flow of Allied forces north.

The fighting along the area from Eindhoven to Uden quickly became known as the fight for Hell's Highway, and the courage of the soldiers on both sides is the stuff of legends. The story of the battle for Hell's Highway is one of the most dramatic of World War II, with lightly armed U.S. paratroopers fighting deadly battles against German tanks and assault guns. This was recognized by Lieutenant General Horrocks at a ceremony on October 30, 1944:

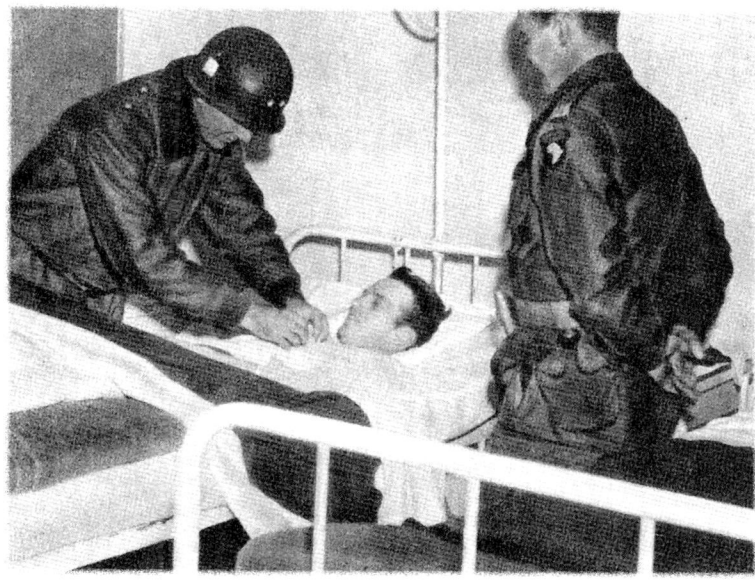

Major General Maxwell Taylor visits the wounded in a hospital in October 1944. *U.S. Army photo*

> *It is a very great honor and privilege for me to give these decorations to members of the one oh first. Your division is surrounded here by British formations and every man of them considers it an honor to have you here. . . . We will be sorry when you go, though I know you'll be glad to leave. I have commanded Four Corps and have never seen a better fighting division than the one oh first. If it hadn't been for you we'd never have been here as quickly as we were. . . . You men of the one oh first have lived up to the very highest traditions of the United States.*

General Maxwell Taylor stands at attention during a 101st Airborne Division awards ceremony in October 1944. *U.S. Army photo*

The German attacks along Hell's Highway had an ominous effect on the advance of XXX Corps. As the Germans attacked and cut the main highway between Veghel and St. Oedenrode, and took up a defensive position astride the road, effectively cutting Hell's Highway, XXX Corps had to send vital combat power back to help the lightly armed 101st and 82nd Airborne divisions. The Screaming Eagles, aided by British tanks, counterattacked German forces in a seesaw battle for control of Hell's Highway. Eventually, the Screaming Eagles and their British allies wrested control of Hell's Highway from the Germans, but the damage was done and valuable time had been lost.

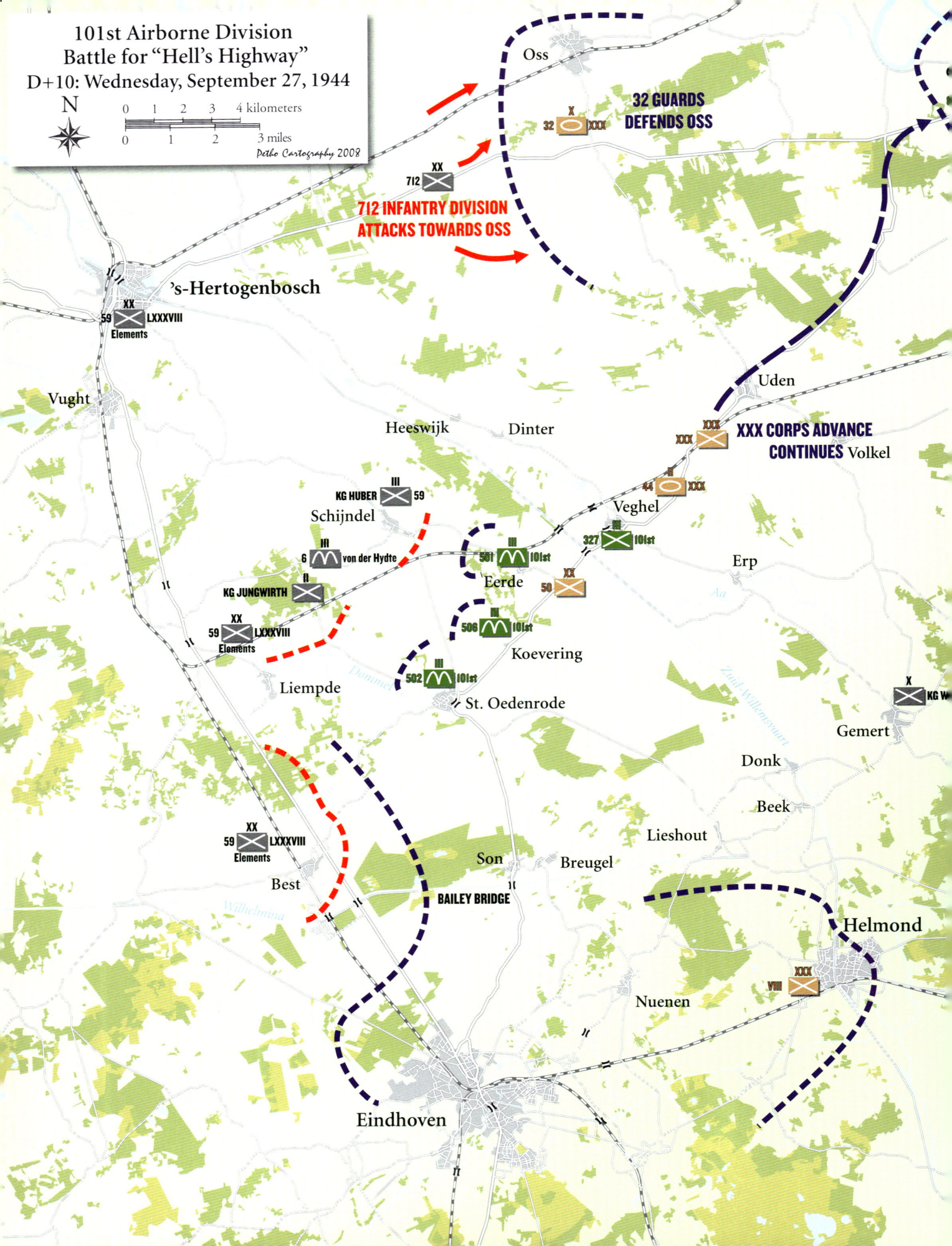

101st Airborne Division
Battle for "Hell's Highway"
D+10: Wednesday, September 27, 1944

N

0 1 2 3 4 kilometers
0 1 2 3 miles

Petho Cartography 2008

Oss

32 | X | XXX
32 GUARDS
DEFENDS OSS

712 | XX
712 INFANTRY DIVISION
ATTACKS TOWARDS OSS

's-Hertogenbosch

59 | XX | LXXXVIII
Elements

Vught

Uden

Heeswijk   Dinter

XXX
XXX CORPS ADVANCE
CONTINUES Volkel

KG HUBER | III | 59

Schijndel

44 | XXX

Veghel

6 | III | von der Hydte

327 | III | 101st

Erp

KG JUNGWIRTH | II

501 | III | 101st

59 | XX | LXXXVIII
Elements

Eerde

50 | XX

506 | III | 101st

Koevering

Liempde

502 | III | 101st

St. Oedenrode

KG W | X

Gemert

Donk

Beek

59 | XX | LXXXVIII
Elements

Lieshout

Best

Son   Breugel

BAILEY BRIDGE

Helmond

VIII | XXX

Nuenen

Eindhoven

At Arnhem, the British Airborne ran into a buzz saw of German counterattacks, and the situation rapidly changed from desperate to dire as time and the Germans worked against the British. Outnumbered and outgunned, the brave and lightly armed British paratroopers were unable to hold out against German tanks, assault guns, artillery, and panzergrenadiers. Overwhelmed by elements of several German SS Panzer divisions, thousands of British paratroopers were captured while the rest of the British and Polish Airborne withdrew to friendly lines south of the Rhine.

The official sixtieth anniversary analysis of Operation Market Garden by the British Ministry of Defense aptly stated the risk and costs of the attack:

The cost of Operation Market Garden, especially as it failed to achieve its objectives, was very high. The reasons for this failure are myriad and clearly show many of the difficulties involved in mounting successful airborne assaults dependent on rapid relief by ground forces. However, although it is easy in hindsight to say that Market Garden should never have taken place, we must remember the circumstances in which the operation was conceived, planned, and conducted. With the Germans on the retreat, September 1944 was the time for a daring operation to shorten the war, and bold decisions had to be taken quickly if the opportunity was not to be lost. Market Garden was a sensibly conceived plan at the

In an awards ceremony in the fall of 1944, a British general presents an award to a soldier from the 327th Glider Infantry Regiment as Maj. Gen. Maxwell Taylor, commanding general, 101st Airborne Division, looks on. *U.S. Army photo*

The story of the battle for Hell's Highway is one of the most dramatic of World War II, with lightly armed U.S. paratroopers fighting deadly battles against German tanks and assault guns. *Brothers in Arms: Hell's Highway screenshot*

Although Operation Market Garden was over by September 25, 1944, the 101st Airborne had to face many more weeks of deadly fighting before they were removed from the line. *Brothers in Arms: Hell's Highway screenshot*

right time, but it was ultimately a plan flawed in too many ways to be a success.

A German assessment conducted after the war agreed that Operation Market Garden was a worthy gamble. In this report, the German officers stated: "The air landings at Eindhoven, Nijmegen, and Arnhem in September 1944 were directed at breaking up the German front and paving the way for the British troops to reach the northern flank of the Ruhr area via the Meuse, the Waal, and the lower Rhine rivers. The plan of attack offered the best chances of a major strategic victory."

In the minds of the Allied commanders who led the operation, and in the views of the enemy who opposed it, the Allied airborne attack in Holland was a worthy gamble. Because Operation Market Garden failed to reach its objective of ending the war in 1944, it is also one of the great "what ifs" of World War II.

Although an operational failure, Market Garden was not without strategic benefit to the Allied cause. The Allied attack in Holland forced the Germans to spend precious resources on the defense of the Netherlands and provided the Allies a foothold from which to launch future drives into Germany. If the bold plan had succeeded, the war might have been ended by Christmas 1944 and millions of lives might have been saved. As it was, the operation was a daring strategic maneuver that failed and the war dragged on until May 8, 1945. That failure cost the U.S. Army serious casualties:

> *The 82nd had lost 1,432 killed and missing, and the 101st sustained 2,110 casualties. The fighting for the two U.S. Airborne divisions did not, however, end with the halt of the drive toward Arnhem. The Allies, faced with continued German pressure against the Market Garden salient, kept the two U.S. divisions in the line. Brigadier General James M. Gavin's 82nd finally started withdrawing on 11 November, after incurring an additional 1,682 casualties; beginning on 25 November Maj. Gen. Maxwell D. Taylor's 101st would follow, having suffered 1,912 more losses.*[5]

Nevertheless, the veterans who fought in Operation Market Garden, and in particular the soldiers of the 101st Airborne Division who battled along Hell's Highway, will tell you that their effort was important. The invasion of Holland liberated a large portion of the Netherlands and drove the battle lines ever closer to Germany. The battle for Hell's Highway had been an important part of this effort. As a result, the battle for Hell's Highway is a story worthy of study, for it proved what a courageous and outnumbered band of paratroopers could accomplish against terrible odds.

Professor Eduardo Peniche, 101st Airborne Market Garden veteran, on October 22, 2007. At this ceremony he was awarded his second Purple Heart, sixty-two years after he was wounded during the Battle of the Bulge. A native of Yucatan, Mexico, he served his adoptive country heroically in World War II and became a U.S. citizen in 1953. A trained linguist in five languages, he retired in 1998 from his position as professor of Spanish at Kingwood College in Texas. He received many awards and honors for both his military service and his work as an educator. He passed away on August 16, 2008, while surrounded by family and friends. (For a description of Peniche in the battle for Hell's Highway, see sidebar on page 77.) *Author photo*

Appendix A

101st Airborne Division Order of Battle for Operation Market Garden

101ST U.S. AIRBORNE DIVISION "SCREAMING EAGLES," MAJ. GEN. MAXWELL TAYLOR

101st Headquarters Company

501st Parachute Infantry Regiment, Colonel Johnson
1st Battalion, Lieutenant Colonel Kinnard
2nd Battalion, Lieutenant Colonel Ballard
3rd Battalion, Lieutenant Colonel Ewell

502nd Parachute Infantry Regiment, Colonel Michaelis
1st Battalion, Lieutenant Colonel Cassidy
2nd Battalion, Lieutenant Colonel Chapman
3rd Battalion, Lieutenant Colonel Cole

506th Parachute Infantry Regiment, Colonel Sink
1st Battalion, Lieutenant Colonel LaPrade
2nd Battalion, Lieutenant Colonel Strayer
3rd Battalion, Lieutenant Colonel Horton

327th Glider Infantry Regiment, Colonel Harper
1st Battalion, Lieutenant Colonel Sallee
2nd Battalion, Lieutenant Colonel Rouzie
*3rd Battalion (1st Battalion, 401st Glider Infantry Regiment), Lieutenant Colonel Allen

Divisional Artillery, Brigadier General McAuliffe
321st Glider Artillery Battalion, Lieutenant Colonel Carmichael
907th Glider Field Artillery Battalion, Lieutenant Colonel Nelson
377th Parachute Field Artillery Battalion, Lieutenant Colonel Elkins
81st Airborne Artillery Antitank Battalion, Lieutenant Colonel Cox

326th Airborne Engineer Battalion, Lieutenant Colonel Pappas

326th Airborne Medical Company, Barfield

426th Airborne Quartermaster Company

Signal Company, Recon Platoon, Military Police Platoon

*Though carried as the 3rd Battalion, 327th Glider Infantry, and considered such by the command, this battalion was actually the 1st Battalion, 401st Glider Infantry, which accounts for the presence within the one regiment of two battalions with A, B, C letter companies. This battalion had served as the 3rd Battalion of the regiment since the Normandy landing.

Appendix B

101st Airborne Division in World War II

COMMAND STAFF

Commanding Generals
15 Sep 43   Maj. Gen. William C. Lee
14 Mar 44   Brig. Gen. Maxwell D. Taylor
31 May 44   Maj. Gen. Maxwell D. Taylor
5 Dec 44   Brig. Gen. Anthony C. McAuliffe
27 Dec 44   Maj. Gen. Maxwell D. Taylor

Assistant Division Commanders
15 Sep 43   Brig. Gen. Don F. Pratt
1 Aug 44   Brig. Gen. Gerald J. Higgins

Artillery Commanders
15 Sep 43   Brig. Gen. Anthony C. McAuliffe
5 Dec 44   Col. Thomas L. Sherburne
27 Dec 44   Brig. Gen. Anthony McAuliffe
9 Feb 45   Col. William N. Gillmore
1 May 45   Brig. Gen. William N. Gillmore

Chiefs of Staff
15 Sep 43   Col. Gerald J. Higgins
11 Aug 44   Lt. Col. Raymond D. Millener
21 Oct 44   Col. Raymond D. Millener
8 Dec 44   Lt. Col. Ned D. Moore (Acting)
28 Dec 44   Col. John H. Michaelis
10 Feb 45   Lt. Col. Ned D. Moore
8 Mar 45   Col. Ned D. Moore

Assistant Chiefs of Staff G-1
15 Sep 43   Lt. Col. Ned D. Moore
14 Dec 44   Maj. Frank R. Brower, Jr. (acting)
28 Dec 44   Lt. Col. Ned D. Moore
10 Feb 45   Maj. Frank R. Brower, Jr.
16 Apr 45   Lt. Col. Frank R. Brower, Jr.

Assistant Chiefs of Staff G-2
15 Sep 43   Lt. Col. Ralph M. Neal
17 Apr 44   Maj. Arthur M. Sommerfield
7 Jul 44   Maj. Paul A. Danahy
11 Nov 44   Lt. Col. Paul A. Danahy

Assistant Chiefs of Staff G-3
15 Sep 43   Lt. Col. Raymond D. Millener
1 Jul 44   Lt. Col. Harold W. Hannah
30 Sep 44   Lt. Col. Harry W. O. Kinnard, Jr.
8 Mar 45   Lt. Col. Charles H. Chase (Acting)
16 Apr 45   Col. Harry W. O. Kinnard, Jr.

Assistant Chiefs of Staff G-4
15 Sep 43   Lt. Col. Carl W. Kohls

Assistant Chiefs of Staff G-5
6 May 44   Maj. Glen C. Eberle
18 Jun 44   Maj. Charles H. Stephens
30 Aug 44   Maj. Ralph L. Blanchard
9 Jan 45   Capt. Robert S. Smith
7 Mar 45   Maj. George R. Dessaussure
7 May 45   Maj. Robert S. Smith

Adjutant General
15 Sep 43   Lt. Col. Edward Schmitt

Commanding Officers, 327th Glider Infantry
15 Sep 43   Col. George S. Wear
10 Jun 44   Col. Joseph H. Harper

Commanding Officers, 501st Parachute Infantry
1 Feb 44   Col. Howard R. Johnson
7 Oct 44   Col. Julian J. Ewell
9 Jan 45   Lt. Col. Robert A. Ballard
30 Apr 45   Col. Robert A. Ballard

Commanding Officers, 502nd Parachute Infantry
15 Sep 43   Col. George V. H. Moseley
9 Jun 44   Col. J. H. Michaelis
23 Sep 44   Col. Steve A. Chappuis

Commanding Officers, 506th Parachute Infantry
15 Sep 43   Col. Robert F. Sink

STATISTICS

Chronology

Activated	15 Aug 1942
Arrived ETO	15 Sept 1943
Arrived Continent (D-Day)	6 June 1944
Entered Combat	6 June 1944
Days in Combat	214

Casualties (Tentative)

Killed	2,043
Wounded	7,976
Missing	1,193
Captured	336
Battle Casualties	11,548

Campaigns

Normandy
Ardennes
Rhineland
Central Europe

Individual Awards

Distinguished Service Cross	47
Legion of Merit	12
Silver Star	516
Soldiers Medal	4
Bronze Star	6,977
Air Medal	46

Prisoners of War Taken	**29,527**

Composition

502nd Parachute Infantry
506th Parachute Infantry
    [assigned in 1 Mar 45 reorganization]
327th Glider Infantry
401st Glider Infantry
    [disbanded in 1 Mar 45 reorganization]
101st Parachute Maintenance Battalion
326th Airborne Engineer Battalion
326th Airborne Medical Company
81st Airborne Antiaircraft Artillery Battalion
101st Airborne Division Artillery
321st Glider Field Artillery Battalion
377th Parachute Field Artillery Battalion
463rd Parachute Field Artillery Battalion
    [assigned in 1 Mar 45 reorganization]
907th Glider Field Artillery Battalion

Special Troops

801st Ordnance Company
426th Quartermaster Company
101st Signal Company
Military Police Platoon
Headquarters Company
Reconnaissance Platoon
Band [assigned in 1 Mar 45 reorganization]

Headquarters special troops activated 1 Mar 45.
    Units previously directly under division.

ATTACHMENTS

Antiaircraft Artillery

1st Plat, Btry A, 474th AAA AW Bn (SP)	9 Jun 44–11 Jun 44
Br 502nd Light AA Btry	[?]–14 Nov 44
2 plats, Co B, 796th AAA AW Bn (SP)	9 Jan 45–10 Jan 45
Btrys A, B & C, 61st Abn AA Bn	11 Jan 45–27 Feb 45
567th AAA AW Bn (Mbl)	23 Feb 45–27 Feb 45
2nd Plat, Btry D, 910th AAA AW Bn (Mbl)	5 May 45–9 May 45

Armored

Co D, 70th Tk Bn	6 Jun 44–16 Jun 44
Co F, 70th Tk Bn	7 Jun 44–[?]
1st Bn, 66th Armd Regt (2nd Armd Div)	17 Jun 44–26 Jun 44
759th Tk Bn	28 Jun 44–8 Jul 44
Br 44th Armd Regt (Br 4th Armd Bde)	19 Sep 44–25 Sep 44
Br 13/18 Hussars (Br 79th Armd Div)	18 Oct 44–22 Oct 44

Br 4/7 Dragoon Guards (Br 79th Armd Div)	2 Nov 44–11 Nov 44
2nd Tk Bn (9th Armd Div)	19 Dec 44–30 Dec 44
CC R (9th Armd Div)	20 Dec 44–31 Dec 44
CC B (10th Armd Div)	20 Dec 44–18 Jan 45
CC B (4th Armd Div)	8 Jan 45–10 Jan 45
Co A & 1st Plat, Co D, 781st Tk Bn	26 Jan 45–28 Jan 45
Co A, 47th Tk Bn (14th Armd Div)	5 Feb 45–14 Feb 45
Co A & 3rd Plat, Co D, 781st Tk Bn	6 Feb 45–7 Feb 45
1st Plat, Co D, 47th Tk Bn (14th Armd Div)	7 Feb 45–13 Feb 45
2nd Plat, Co D, 47th Tk Bn (14th Armd Div)	13 Feb 45–19 Feb 45
Co B, 47th Tk Bn (14th Armd Div)	14 Feb 45–25 Feb 45
113th Tk Bn	5 May 45–8 May 45
774th Tk Bn	5 May 45–9 May 45

Cavalry

24th Cav Rcn Sq	29 Jun 44–8 Jul 44
4th Cav Gp	1 Jul 44–8 Jul 44
Br 53rd Rcn Regt (Br 53rd Div)	5 Oct 44–6 Oct 44
Sqs A & B Br Royal Scots Greys	6 Oct 44–7 Oct 44
Br 61st Rcn Regt	6 Oct 44–12 Oct 44
Sq C Br Royal Scots Greys	6 Oct 44–17 Oct 44
Sq C Br 61st Rcn Regt	10 Oct 44–12 Oct 44
Br 53rd Rcn Regt (Br 53rd Div)	13 Oct 44–19 Oct 44
101st Cav Gp	5 May 45–9 May 45
116th Cav Rcn Sq	8 May 45–9 May 45

Chemical

Cos B & C, 87th Cml Mort Bn	11 Jun 44–12 Jun 44
Co B, 99th Cml Mort Bn	5 May 45–8 May 45

Engineer

48th Engr C Bn	5 May 45–9 May 45

Field Artillery

65th Armd FA Bn	6 Jun 44–26 Jun 44
87th Armd FA Bn	10 Jun 44–14 Jun 44
188th FA Bn (155 how)	11 Jun 44–12 Jun 44
951st FA Bn (155 how)	12 Jun 44–15 Jun 44
14th FA Abn Bn	13 Jun 44–16 Jun 44
Br 4th Royal Horse Field Arty Regt (RA) (Mecz)	12 Oct 44–18 Oct 44
Br 147th Field Arty Regt	18 Oct 44–[?]
Br 6th Field Arty Regt	8 Nov 44–[?]
463rd Prcht FA Bn	18 Dec 44–[?]
755th FA Bn (155 how)	19 Dec 44–12 Jan 45
969th FA Bn (155 how)	19 Dec 44–12 Jan 45
775th FA Bn (4.5-inch gun)	19 Dec 44–15 Jan 45
333rd FA Gp	20 Dec 44–28 Dec 44
559th FA Bn (155 gun)	1 Jan 45–3 Jan 45
559th FA Bn (155 gun)	11 Jan 45–12 Jan 45
687th FA Bn (105 how)	12 Jan 45–18 Jan 45
770th FA Bn (4.5-inch gun)	13 Jan 45–14 Jan 45

463rd Prcht FA Bn	25 Feb 45–26 Feb 45
250th FA Gp	7 Apr 45–11 Apr 45
790th FA Bn (80-inch how)	7 Apr 45–11 Apr 45
942nd FA Bn (155 how)	7 Apr 45–17 Apr 45
490th FA Bn (155 how)	10 Apr 45–17 Apr 45
805th FA Bn (155 how)	12 Apr 45–17 Apr 45
529th FA Bn (8-inch how)	14 Apr 45–17 Apr 45
791st FA Bn (8-inch how)	15 Apr 45–17 Apr 45
969th FA Bn (155 how)	5 May 45–7 May 45
522nd FA Bn (105 how)	5 May 45–7 May 45
342nd Armd FA Bn	8 May 45–9 May 45

Infantry

506th Prcht Inf	15 Sep 43–becomes organic 1 Mar 45
501st Prcht Inf	Jan 44–still attached 9 May 45
Br 5th Duke of Cornwall's Light Inf	5 Oct 44–[?]
Br Sherwood Rangers	22 Oct 44–2 Nov 44
Br Sherwood Rangers	2 Nov 44–[?]
Br 152nd Brig (51st Highland Div)	19 Nov 44–26 Nov 44
509th Prcht Inf Bn (Non–Div)	22 Nov 44–18 Dec 44
Task Force Higgins	3 Jan 45–6 Jan 45
193rd Gli Inf (17th Abn Div)	3 Jan 45–7 Jan 45
193rd Gli Inf (17th Abn Div)	14 Jan 45–18 Jan 45

Tank Destroyer

Br 304th AT Btry	12 Oct 44–13 Oct 44
Br 74th AT Btry	9 Nov 44–13 Nov 44
705th TD Bn (SP)	20 Dec 44–18 Jan 45
Co B, 811th TD Bn (SP)	3 Jan 45–11 Jan 45
Cos B & C, 705th TD Bn (SP)	3 Jan 45–11 Jan 45
Co C (– 1 plat), 704th TD Bn (SP)	4 Jan 45–6 Jan 45
Co A, 602nd TD Bn (SP)	4 Jan 45–6 Jan 45
611th TD Bn	6 Jan 45–7 Jan 45
Co B (– 1 plat), 704th TD Bn (SP)	9 Jan 45–11 Jan 45
Co C, 609th TD Bn (SP)	11 Jan 45–12 Jan 45
807th TD Bn (SP)	20 Jan 45–25 Feb 45
813th TD Bn (SP)	5 May 45–9 May 45

Navy

| Prov Abn Naval Shore Fire Control Parties | 16 May 44–[?] |

DETACHMENTS (ATTACHED TO)

Antiaircraft Artillery

| Btrys D, E & F, 81st Abn AA Bn | VII Corps | 6 Jun 44–11 Jun 44 |

Field Artillery

| 377th Prcht FA Bn | 100th Div | 25 Jan 45–28 Jan 45 |

Infantry

2nd Bn, 401st Gli Inf	82nd Abn Div	6 Jun 44–1 Mar 45
502nd Prcht Inf	82nd Abn Div	4 Oct 44–5 Oct 44
506th Prcht Inf	4th Div	2 May 45–3 May 45

ASSIGNMENT AND ATTACHMENT TO HIGHER UNITS
(* RELIEVED FROM ASSIGNMENT)

DATE	CORPS	ARMY Assigned	Attached	ARMY GROUP Assigned	Attached
21 Aug 43	V			ETOUSA	
22 Oct 43	*		First		
22 Jan 44	VIII		First		
13 Mar 44		First	*		
6 Jun 44	VII	First			
15 Jun 44	VIII	First			
15 Jul 44	*	*	Ninth		
12 Aug 44	XVIII Abn	First Allied Abn	*		
18 Sep 44	Br XXX	First Allied Abn	Br Second		
21 Sep 44	Br I ABN	First Allied Abn	Br Second		
23 Sep 44	Br VIII	First Allied Abn	Br Second		
28 Sep 44	Br XII	First Allied Abn	Br Second		
9 Nov 44	Cdn II	First Allied Abn	Cdn First		
17 Dec 44	VIII	First Allied Abn	Third		12th
21 Dec 44	VIII	First Allied Abn	Third		12th
26 Dec 44	III	First Allied Abn	Third		12th
29 Dec 44	VIII	First Allied Abn	Third		12th
19 Jan 45	*	First Allied Abn	Third		12th
20 Jan 45	XV	First Allied Abn	Seventh		6th
26 Jan 45	VI Opns	First Allied Abn	Seventh (Adm&Sup)		6th
28 Feb 45	XVIII Abn	First Allied Abn	*	*	*
1 Apr 45	XXII	First Allied Abn	Fifteenth		12th
6 Apr 45	*	First Allied Abn			12th
17 Apr 45	XVIII Abn	First Allied Abn	Seventh		6th
23 Apr 45	VI	First Allied Abn	Seventh		6th
4 May 45	XXI	First Allied Abn	Seventh		6th

COMMAND POSTS

DATE	TOWN	REGION	COUNTRY
15 Sep 43	Liverpool	Lancashire	England
15 Sep 43	Newbury (Greenham Lodge)	Berkshire	England
6 Jun 44	Hiesville	Manche	France
12 Jun 44	Carentan	Manche	France
27 Jun 44	St. Saveur-le-Vicomte	Manche	France
29 Jun 44	Cherbourg (5 mi S)	Manche	France
15 Jul 44	Newbury (Greenham Lodge)	Berkshire	England
17 Sep 44	Zon	Nord Brabant	Netherlands
20 Sep 44	St. Oedenrode	Nord Brabant	Netherlands
24 Sep 44	Vechel	Nord Brabant	Netherlands
5 Oct 44	Slik Ewjik	Nord Brabant	Netherlands
1 Dec 44	Mourmelon	Marne	France
18 Dec 44	Mande St. Etienne	Luxembourg	Belgium
19 Dec 44	Bastogne	Luxembourg	Belgium
7 Jan 45	Isle-le-Pre	Luxembourg	Belgium
21 Jan 45	Drulingen	Bas-Rhin	France
25 Jan 45	Hochfelden	Bas-Rhin	France
28 Feb 45	Mourmelon	Marne	France
1 Apr 45	Glehn	Rhineland	Germany
24 Apr 45	Merchingen	Wurttemberg	Germany
27 Apr 45	Memmingen	Bavaria	Germany
1 May 45	Kaufbeuren	Bavaria	Germany
2 May 45	Wolfratshausen	Bavaria	Germany
4 May 45	Miesbach	Bavaria	Germany

Appendix C

British Order of Battle for Market Garden

21ST ARMY GROUP
Field Marshal Montgomery

2ND BRITISH ARMY
Lieutenant General Dempsey

BRITISH XXX CORPS
Lieutenant General Horrocks

2ND HOUSEHOLD CAVALRY REGT
Guards Armoured Division—Major General Adair

- **5th Guards Brigade—Brigadier General Gwatkin**
  - 2nd Armoured Battalion Grenadier Guards (Shermans)
  - 2nd Armoured Battalion Irish Guards (Shermans)
  - 1st Motor Battalion Grenadier Guards (Half-tracked infantry)
  - 3rd Battalion Irish Guards (Lorried infantry)
- **32nd Guards Brigade—Brigadier General Johnson**
  - 1st Armoured Battalion Coldstream Guards (Shermans)
  - 2nd Armoured Recce Battalion Welsh Guards (Cromwells)
  - 5th Battalion Coldstream Guards (Lorried infantry)
  - 1st Battalion Welsh Guards (Lorried infantry)
- **Divisional Artillery**
  - 55th Field Regiment
  - 153rd (Leicestershire Yeomanry) Field Regiment
  - 21st Antitank Regiment
  - 94th Light Anti-Air Regiment

43RD (WESSEX) DIVISION— MAJOR GENERAL THOMAS

- **69th Infantry Brigade**
  - 5th Battalion East Yorkshire Regiment
  - 6th Battalion Green Howards
  - 7th Battalion Green Howards
- **151st Infantry Brigade**
  - 6th Battalion Durham Light Infantry
  - 8th Battalion Durham Light Infantry
  - 9th Battalion Durham Light Infantry
- **231st Infantry Brigade**
  - 2nd Battalion Devonshire Regiment
  - 1st Battalion Hampshire Regiment
  - 1st Battalion Dorsetshire Regiment
- **Divisional Artillery**
  - 74th Field Regiment
  - 90th Field Regiment (SP)
  - 124th Field Regiment
  - 102nd Anti-Tank Regiment (Northumberland Hussars)
  - 25th Light Anti-Aircraft Regiment
- **Divisional Troops**
  - 61st Recce Regiment
  - 2nd Battalion Chesire (MMG)

50TH (NORTHUMBRIAN) DIVISION— MAJOR GENERAL GRAHAM

8th Armoured Brigade—Brigadier Prior-Palmer

- 4/7th Royal Dragoon Guards
- 13/18th Hussars
- Nottinghamshire Yeomanry (Sherwood Rangers)
- 12th Battalion King's Royal Rifle Corps (Motor)

Royal Netherlands Brigade "Prinses Irene"

XII CORPS
Lieutenant General Ritchie

7th Armoured Division

15th (Scottish) Division

53rd (Welch) Division

VIII CORPS
Lieutenant General O'Conner

11th Armoured Division

3rd Division

4th Armored Brigade

1st Belgian Brigade

Notes

CHAPTER 1
1. Perkins, *Mission Accomplished: A Story in Words and Pictures of the 321st Glider Field Artillery Battalion in World War II.*

CHAPTER 2
1. Perkins.
2. Ibid.

CHAPTER 3
1. Perkins.

CHAPTER 4
1. Marshall and Westover, "101st Airborne Division, September 1944, Operation Market Report."
2. "Tactical Operations of the 101st Market Garden Operation."
3. Marshall and Westover.
4. Pogue, *United States Army in World War II: European Theater of Operations*, 284–286.
5. Ibid., 286.
6. Perkins.

CHAPTER 5
1. Marshall and Westover.
2. Ibid.
3. Warren, *Airborne Operations in World War II: European Theater*, 118.
4. Ibid., 123–124.

CHAPTER 6
1. Ballard, "The U.S. Army Campaigns of World War II: Rhineland."
2. Warren, 128–130.

CHAPTER 7
1. *Army Intelligence Bulletin*, October 1944. (Information collected in July and August 1944.)
2. *Military Intelligence Service Bulletin*, January 1943.
3. Warren, 136.

CHAPTER 8
1 "Combat Lessons, Number 6: Street Fighting." (Derived from lessons learned in combat in 1944.)
2. Warren, 136.

CHAPTER 9
1. Warren, 140–141.
2. Ibid., 140.
3. Perkins.
4. Warren, 140.
5. Marshall and Westover.
6. 327th GIR S-3 periodic reports, 18 September to 27 November, inclusive.

CHAPTER 10
1. Warren, 141.
2. *Army Intelligence Bulletin*, June 1944.
3. Perkins.

CHAPTER 11
1. *Army Intelligence Bulletin*, October 1944. (From information collected in July and August 1944.)
2. Pogue, 288.

CHAPTER 12
1. Warren, 145.
2. Pogue, 287.
3. Ibid., 288.
4. MacDonald, *The European Theater of Operations, The Siegfried Line Campaign*, 195.
5. Koskimaki, *Hell's Highway: Chronicle of the 101st Airborne Division in the Holland Campaign*, 315–316.

CHAPTER 13
1. MacDonald, "The Decision to Launch Operation Market Garden."
2. Horrocks, *A Full Life*, 232.
3. Ibid.
4. Linda Chauvin, daughter of 1st Lt. Eugene P. Shauvin, interview with the author, 2006.
5. Ballard.

Glossary

101st Airborne Division "Screaming Eagles": Activated on August 15, 1942, the 101st Airborne Division became one of the most famous units in the European theater of operations during World War II. The 101st Airborne arrived in England September 15, 1943, and received additional training in Berkshire and Wiltshire. On June 6, 1944, the division was dropped into Normandy behind Utah Beach. Against fierce resistance it took Pouppeville, Vierville, and St. Come du Mont. On the 12th, the stronghold of Carentan fell, and after mopping up and maintaining its positions, the division returned to England on July 13 for rest and training. On September 17, 1944, the Screaming Eagles took part in one of the largest airborne invasions in history, Operation Market Garden, and landed behind German lines in the Netherlands (Holland). The Screaming Eagles took their objectives and then battled the Germans along Hell's Highway from September 17–26, 1944.

Amis: German slang for Americans.

Arbeitseinsatz: German term for the drafting of laborers from the occupied countries to fill in the vacancies in Germany in arms factories, the farming sector, and community services. In 1942, Dutch civilians were drafted across the Netherlands for this forced labor. Every man between the ages of eighteen and forty-five was obliged to leave his home to work in German factories. By 1945, nearly eight million workers were drafted from the occupied countries for forced labor in Germany.

Bailey Bridge: A transportable prefabricated truss bridge that can be carried in trucks and is strong enough to hold tanks. The Bailey was used very effectively by Allied combat engineering units to span gaps up to sixty meters wide during World War II. The Bailey is considered one of the great examples of military engineering, since it requires no special tools or heavy equipment for construction.

Bren carrier: A small, tracked, open-topped, British-designed armored vehicle also known as the universal carrier, used by British forces during World War II.

Bren Gun: The Bren was an extremely effective .303-caliber, 22.8-pound, light machine gun used by the British Commonwealth forces in World War II. The word *Bren* comes from Brno, the Czechoslovak city of design, and Enfield, the location of the British Royal small-arms factory.

C-47: An American-made, two-engine transport aircraft also known as a Skytrain, Dakota, or DC-3. The C-47 was the workhorse of World War II and was used to drop paratroopers, tow gliders, and haul passengers and equipment.

Colour sergeant: The equivalent rank of staff sergeant in the Irish Guards of the British army. The insignia is a crown over three chevrons.

D-Day: The unnamed day on which a particular operation (in this case Normandy) commences or is to commence. D+1 is the second day of the operation; D+2 the third; and so on.

Division: An organizational combat unit generally made up of two or three regiments, or two or more brigades, and usually controlled by a corps. In general, a division would have between ten and twenty thousand soldiers assigned.

DZ: Drop zone. Paratroopers jump into DZs.

Enfilade: A concept in military tactics used to describe a military formation's exposure to "flanking fire." The word comes from French (*enfiler*, to skewer).

Fallschirmjäger: German for paratrooper.

Feldgendarmerie: German field police. These military policemen directed traffic and maintained order and discipline behind the front lines.

Feldwebel: German for sergeant.

FG42: The *Fallschirmjägergewehr* 42 was an 8mm Mauser, 11.2-lb. automatic rifle produced in Germany during World War II. The FG42 was developed specifically for the use by *Fallschirmjägers,* hence its designation as *Fallschirmjägergewehr.* After the horrific fighting during the airborne assault on Crete in 1941, the *Fallschirmjägers* expressed the urgent need for a weapon with more range and firepower. The result was the FG42, which could be used in both semiautomatic and automatic modes. A weapon ahead of its time, it was difficult and expensive to manufacture, and only small numbers were issued during the war.

Firefly: A British Sherman tank that was upgraded from the standard American Sherman Tank with a high-velocity 17-pound (76mm) cannon. The standard M4 Sherman tank was woefully undergunned and was armed with a 75mm cannon that could not penetrate the front or flanks of most of the German tanks in World War II. The 17-pound cannon allowed the Firefly to defeat the German Panzer V (Panther) and Panzer VI (Tiger) tanks.

First sergeant: The chief noncommissioned officer of a company, battery, or troop in the U.S. Army.

Flak (Fliegerabwehrkanone): Antiaircraft artillery. The term *flak* became known by Allied forces to mean anything shot into the air in an air defense role against enemy air units.

G-2: A staff officer responsible for intelligence collection and intelligence operations, normally at the division level. In the U.S. Army, the G-2 is the assistant chief of staff, G-2 (Intelligence) at the division, corps, or army level of command.

Generaloberst: German for colonel general, a rank used by the German military in World War II and equivalent to general in the U.S. Army; the rank before *Generalfeldmarschall* (field marshal).

Hauptscharführer: German SS rank for master sergeant.

Hauptsturmführer: German SS rank for captain. Head storm leader.

Heer: The regular German army formally announced in 1935 and disbanded in August of 1946 by the Allies.

Irish Guards: Originally formed in 1900, the Irish Guards are a unit with a proud heritage in the British army who are affectionately known as "The Micks." The Irish Guards fought in the early battles of World War II, and in June 1941, the 2nd and 3rd battalions landed with the Guards Armored Division in Normandy and fought with them until the end of the war, taking part in the advance from the Seine to Nijmegen. It was just before Operation Market Garden that Lt. Col. J. O. E. Vandeleur, commander of the Irish Guards, led an attack on the bridge over the Meuse-Escaut Canal at De Groote Barrier (as explained in the film *A Bridge Too Far* with Vandeleur played by the actor Michael Caine). This bridge is known today as "Joe's Bridge" to honor Vandeleur and the exploits of his Irish Guards. During Operation Market Garden, the Irish Guards worked closely with the 101st Airborne Division to keep Hell's Highway open for the British XXX Corps.

Jabo: A German term derived from the German "Jaeger-bomber," or "fighter-bomber" (literally, "hunter-bomber").

Jaeger: German rank of private in the *Fallschirmjägers* (paratroopers).

Jawohl: German for "Yes sir."

Kampfgruppe: This German term refers to a flexible combat formation of company to brigade size. They were banded together temporarily to perform a specific task and formed from many different types of military units that were required or available.

Leutnant: German for *lieutenant.*

Luftwaffe: German air force. The *Fallschirmjäger* (German paratroopers) were officially assigned to the *Luftwaffe,* not the *Wehrmacht* (German army), but received direction, combat support, and logistics from the regular *Wehrmacht.*

LZ: The military abbreviation for landing zone. Gliders landed in LZs.

Maschinengewehr 42: German for *machine gun 42* or MG42. The MG42 was a superb, fast-firing machine gun that entered service with German forces in 1942. The 7.92mm (8mm Mauser) –caliber weapon was one of the fastest firing (1,200 rounds per minute) and most effective machine guns ever made.

MP40: The MP40, often called the Schmeisser or "burp gun" by the Americans, was a highly effective 9mm submachine gun used by the *Wehrmacht* during World War II. The MP40 (*Maschinenpistole* 40, literally means machine pistol 40) was used extensively by *Fallschirmjägers,* squad leaders, and platoon leaders. The MP40 was very effective in close combat and had an effective range of about thirty meters. The MP40 had a folding metal stock and a thirty-two-round detachable magazine.

Oberfeldwebel: German for master sergeant, a senior sergeant who usually led a section (sixteen to twenty soldiers) or platoon (between thirty and fifty soldiers). *Herr Oberfeldwebel* is the proper official greeting and literally means Mr. Master Sergeant.

Oberjaeger: German rank of corporal in the *Fallschirmjäger* (German paratroopers).

Oberstleutnant: German for *lieutenant colonel.* A lieutenant colonel usually commanded a battalion or battle group of anywhere between one and eight hundred men.

Obersturmführer: The rank of first lieutenant in the World War II German SS. It literally means head storm leader.

P-47: The P-47 Thunderbolt was one of the main U.S. Army Air Force (USAAF) fighters of World War II. Also known as the Jug, the aircraft was the largest single-engine fighter of its day and was especially effective in the ground-attack missions.

PAN: A Dutch resistance group, "Partisan Action Netherlands," in Eindhoven that was established in 1943 and had nearly a hundred members. Consisting mostly of young, idealistic men and women, PAN operated in the Eindhoven, Netherlands, area.

Panzerfaust: German for a light, portable antitank grenade launcher. Literally translated as *tank fist,* the panzerfaust was a lethal and important antitank weapon. The panzerfaust 30 was the most common version of the panzerfaust in September 1944, which had a warhead that could penetrate 200mm of armor and had a range of thirty meters.

Panzergrenadier: German for mechanized or armored infantry. The term *panzergrenadier* was adopted in 1942 and applied equally to both the infantry component of panzer divisions as well as the new divisions known as panzergrenadier divisions. Organized as combined arms formations, panzergrenadier units employed infantry, usually mounted in half-tracks, and mechanized artillery working closely with tanks. Armored infantry. Many panzergrenadier units used trucks because German industry was incapable of producing sufficient half-tracks for all panzergrenadier units. Panzergrenadier were assigned to panzer divisions. As the war dragged on and attrition ate away at the German army, panzergrenadier units more often fought as foot infantry.

PPSh-41 submachine gun: A Russian-made submachine gun. The PPSh-41 (Pistolet-Pulemet Shpagina) was a simple and durable weapon that was produced in great numbers by the Russians during World War II. The submachine gun used the 7.62mm x 25mm pistol round and could hold either a drum magazine containing seventy-one rounds or stick magazines containing thirty-five rounds.

Stadia reticle: Targeting reticule used by bazookas and *Panzerfaust* antitank weapons that employed a stadiametric range estimation based on the average sizes of armored fighting vehicles.

Sten gun: A British 9mm submachine gun. The Sten was an open-bolt, blowback-operated, selective-fire firearm developed at low cost and very effective at close range. STEN is an acronym, cited as derived from the names of the weapon's chief designers, Maj. Reginald Shepherd and Harold Turpin, and EN for Enfield. More than four million Sten guns were produced during World War II. The Sten had a side-feeding magazine that was a direct copy of the German MP40 submachine gun magazine.

Sturmbannführer: The rank of major in the German SS.

Sturmgeschütz or StuG: German for *assault gun,* usually abbreviated StuG. These turretless assault guns provided fire support for infantry, panzer, and panzergrenadier units. The StuG was a tank chassis with a gun, usually a long-barreled 75mm, directly mounted on it. It was cheaper and easier to build than a turreted tank and therefore was produced in great numbers. Due to not having a turret, the StuG had a low profile, heavy frontal armor, and a large cannon, usually a high-velocity 75mm. The StuG had a crew of four.

Top: U.S. Army slang for *first sergeant.* The first sergeant is the "top" sergeant of a company.

Typhoon fighter-bomber: The Hawker Typhoon was a British single-seat fighter-bomber, developed in 1941, that was armed with four 20mm cannons and could carry two 1,000-pound bombs or eight RP3 60-pound warhead unguided rockets. The Typhoon became one of the most successful ground-attack aircraft during World War II and was used with great effect along Hell's Highway during Operation Market Garden.

Waffen-SS: The *Waffen-SS,* or fighting *SS,* were a separate army in the German military that had different ranks and were dedicated to furthering the Nazi cause. The *Waffen-SS* was a frontline fighting organization with nearly half a million soldiers by the end of World War II. Most units of the *Waffen-SS* fought with fierce bitterness against the Allies and civilian populations and were responsible for several notorious war crimes during World War II. At the Nuremberg Trials in 1945, the *Waffen-SS* was condemned as a criminal organization due to their involvement with the National Socialist German Workers Party (Nazi), except conscripts sworn in after 1943, who were exempted from the judgment on the basis of involuntary servitude.

Wehrmacht: German for *armed force* from 1935 to 1945. The *Wehrmacht* consisted of the *Heer* (army), the *Kriegsmarine* (navy), and the *Luftwaffe* (air force). The *Waffen-SS* was not officially part of the *Wehrmacht* but was subject to *Wehrmacht* operational and tactical control.

XXX Corps: The British XXX Corps was an armored (tank heavy) corps in the British army that played a critical role in Operation Market Garden during World War II. XXX Corps was led by Lt. Gen. Brian Horrocks. During Operation Market Garden, XXX Corps had the mission to fight its way up a sixty-mile-long narrow road from the Belgium border through the Netherlands, from Eindhoven to Nijmegen to Arnhem, and then to link up with the airborne forces that had been dropped at strategic bridge and crossing points along the axis of attack.

Bibliography

327th GIR S-3 periodic reports.

After Action Report. Third U.S. Army, 1 August 1944–9 May 1945, 2 vols. Washington, D.C.: U.S. Army Adjutant General, 1945. Includes planning phase as well as the operations.

Airborne History, 1940–1946. Ft. Benning, GA: U.S. Infantry School, 1946.

Airborne Operations: A German Appraisal. Washington, D.C.: Department of the Army, 1951. History Department, Thayer Hall.

Army Intelligence Bulletin, June 1944.

Army Intelligence Bulletin, October 1944.

Ballard, Ted. "The U.S. Army Campaigns of World War II: Rhineland." U.S. Army Center of Military History, CMH Pub 72–25.

Bando, Mark. *Vanguard of the Crusade: The 101st Airborne Division in World War II*. Bedford, PA: Aberjona Press, 2002.

Basset, James A. "Airphibious Warfare." Master's Thesis. Washington, D.C.: Georgetown, 1948.

Biggs, Bradley. *Gavin*. Hamden, Conn.: Archon Book, 1980.

Blair, Clay. *Ridgeway's Paratroopers: The American Airborne in World War II*. Garden City, NY: Dial Press, 1985.

Bowen, Robert M. *Fighting with the Screaming Eagles: With 101st Airborne from Normandy to Bastogne*. Mechanicsburg, PA: Stackpole, 2001.

Bradley, Francis Xavier, and H. Glen Wood. *Paratrooper*. Harrisburg, PA: Stackpole, 1962.

Brereton, Lewis Hyde. *The Brereton Diaries: The War in the Air, in the Pacific, Middle East and Europe, 3 October 1941– 8 May 1945*. New York: W. Morrow and Co., 1946.

Buckeridge, Justin P. *Bolt from the Blue: 550 Infantry Airborne Battalion, 1941–45*. Nashville, TN: Battery Press, 1978.

Burriss, T. Moffatt. *Strike and Hold: A Memoir of the 82nd Airborne in World War II*. Washington, D.C.: Brassey's, 2002.

Cluxton, Donald E., Jr. "Concepts of Airborne Warfare in World War II." Master's Thesis. Chapel Hill, NC: Duke University, 1967.

"Combat Lessons, Number 6: Street Fighting." U.S. Department of War, March 1945.

Craven, Wesley Frank, and James Lea Cate. *Army Air Forces in World War II: Europe: Argument to V-E Day, January 1944 to May 1945*. Chicago: University of Chicago Press, 1951.

Crookenden, Sir Napier. *Airborne at War*. New York: Scribner, 1978.

Devlin, Gerard M. *Paratrooper! The Saga of U.S. Army and Marine Parachute and Glider Combat Troops During World War II*. New York: St. Martin Press, 1979.

——— *Silent Wings: The Saga of U.S. Army and Marine Combat Glider Pilots During World War II*. New York: St. Martin Press, 1985.

Gabel, Kurt. *The Making of a Paratrooper: Airborne Training and Combat in World War II*. Lawrence: University of Kansas, 1990.

Gavin, James M. *Airborne Warfare*. Washington, D.C.: Infantry Journal Press, 1947.

———. *On to Berlin: Battles of an Airborne Commander, 1943–1946*. New York: Viking Press, 1978.

Harclerode, Peter. *Arnhem: A Tragedy of Errors*. London: Arms and Armour, 1994.

Harrison, Gordon A. *European Theater of Operations: Cross-Channel Attack*. Washington, D.C.: Office of the Chief of Military History, 1951.

Horrocks, Lt. Gen. Sir Brian. *A Full Life*. London: Collins, 1960.

Hoyt, Edwin Palmer. *Airborne: The History of American Parachute Forces*. New York: Stein and Day, 1979.

Huston, James Alvin. *United States Army in World War II, Airborne Operations*. Washington, D.C.: Office of the Chief of Military History, History Department, Thayer Hall, 1950.

Jackson, Robert. *Arnhem: The Battle Remembered*. Shrewsbury, U.K.: Airlife Book, 2003.

Koskimaki, George. *D-Day with the Screaming Eagles*. Harrisburg, PA: Stackpole, 2002.

———. *Hell's Highway: Chronicle of the 101st Airborne Division in the Holland Campaign, September–November 1944*. Havertown, PA: Casemate, 2003.

Lee, William C. "Air Infantry." *Infantry Journal* (Jan 1941): pp. 14–21.

Lloyd, Alan. *Gliders*. Nashville, TN: The Battery Press, 1982.

Lucas, James. *Storming Eagles: German Airborne Forces in World War II*. New York: Arms and Armour Press, 1988.

MacDonald, Charles B. "The Decision to Launch Operation Market Garden." *Command Decisions*, Chapter 19, Kent Roberts Greenfield, ed. New York: Harcourt, Brace and Company, Inc., 1959.

———. *The European Theater of Operations, The Siegfried Line Campaign*. Washington, D.C.: Center of Military History, U.S. Army, 1993.

Marshall, Col. S. L. A., and Capt. John G. Westover. "101st Airborne Division, September 1944, Operation Market Report," October 10, 1944.

McDonough, James I. *Sky Riders: History of the 327/401 Glider Infantry*. Nashville, TN: Battery Press, 1980.

Megellas, James. *All the Way to Berlin: The Memoir of an Airborne Platoon Leader*. Novato, CA: Presidio Press, 2002.

Military Intelligence Service Bulletin, January 1943.

Nordyke, Phil. *All American: All the Way: The Combat History of the 82nd Airborne Division in World War II*. St. Paul, MN: Zenith Press, 2005.

O'Donnell, Patrick K. *Beyond Valor: World War II's Rangers and Airborne Veterans Reveal the Heart of Combat in Their Own Words. The Personal Stories of America's World War II Veterans*. Thorndike, ME: Thorndike Press, 2001.

Palgi, Yoel. *Into the Inferno: Memoir of a Jewish Paratrooper Behind Nazi Lines*. Piscataway, NJ: Rutgers University Press, 2002.

Palmer, Robert R., Bell I. Wiley, and William R. Keast. *Army Ground Forces: The Procurement and Training of Ground Combat Troops.* Washington, D.C.: Historical Division, Department of the Army, 1948.

Perkins, Joseph K. *Mission Accomplished, A Story in Words and Pictures of the 321st Glider Field Artillery Battalion in World War II.* Germany, 1945.

Pogue, Forrest C. *United States Army in World War II, European Theater of Operations, The Supreme Command.* Chapter XVI, "Fighting in the North." Washington, D.C.: Office of the Chief of Military History, Department of the Army, 1954.

Ridgeway, Matthew Bunker. *Soldier: The Memoirs of Matthew B. Ridgeway.* New York: Harper & Brothers, 1956.

Ruggero, Ed. *Combat Jump: The Young Men Who Led the Assault into Fortress Europe, July 1943.* New York: Harper Collins, 2003.

Ryan, Cornelius. *A Bridge Too Far.* New York: Simon and Schuster, 1974.

Sampson, Francis L. *Look Out Below! A Story of the Airborne.* Washington, D.C.: The Catholic University of America Press, 1958.

September 1944: Operation Market Garden: A. Korthals Altes. Weesp, Holland: Fibula-Van Dishoeck, 1984.

Sosabowski, Stanislaw. *Freely I Served.* Nashville, TN: Battery Press, 1982.

"Tactical Operations of the 101st Market Garden Operation." 101st Airborne Division Official Records.

Taylor, Maxwell D. *Swords and Plowshares.* New York: W. W. Norton & Co., 1972.

Thompson, Leroy. *U.S. Airborne in Action.* Carrollton, TX: Squadron/Signal Publications, Inc., 1992.

Tugwell, Maurice. *Airborne to Battle: A History of Airborne Warfare, 1918–1971.* London: Kimber, 1971.

United States Army. *Fort Benning, Georgia. Historical and Pictorial Review of the Parachute Battalions, United States Army.* Ft. Benning, GA: 1942.

U.S. War Dept. Field Service Regulations: Operations: Field Manual 100-5, dated June 1944.

Warren, Dr. John C. *Airborne Operations in World War II, European Theater.* USAF Historical Division Research Studies Institute, Air University, September 1956.

Webster, David Kenyon. *Parachute Infantry: An American Paratrooper's Memoir of D-Day and the Fall of the Third Reich.* Baton Rouge: Louisiana State University Press, 1994.

Whiting, Charles. *Hunters from the Sky: The German Parachute Corps, 1940–1945.* London: Leo Cooper, 1974.

Yank: Army Weekly, 1942–1945, reprint edition. New York: Arno Press, 1967.

Yarborough, W. P. "The New Aerial Doughboys," *Pointer* (10 October 1941): 8–11.

Personal Papers
Technical Sergeant Four George Koskimaki
Pfc. Eduardo Peniche

Index

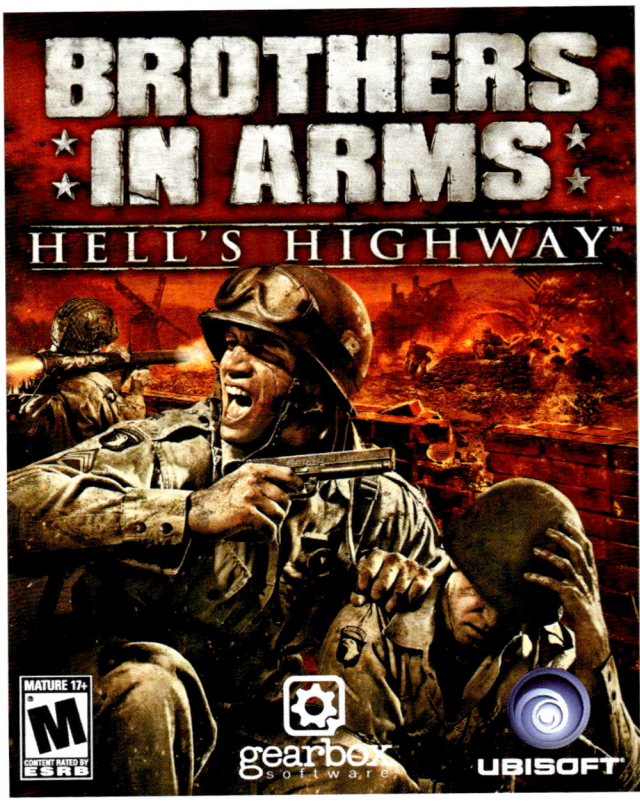
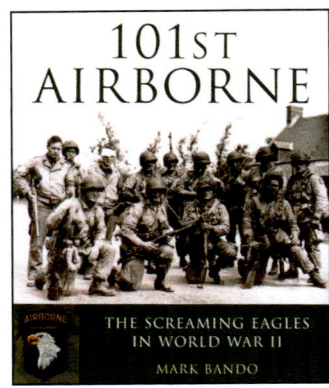
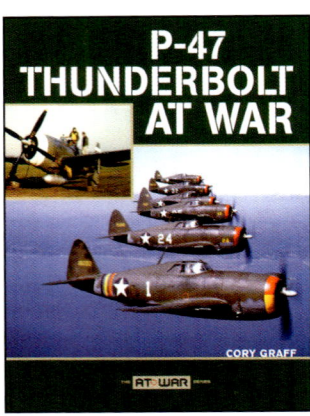
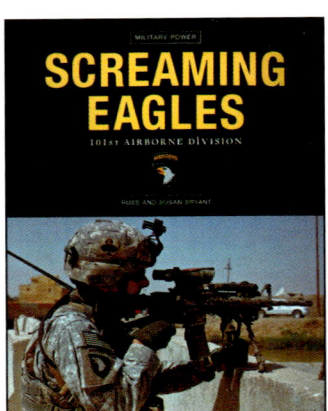